I0797778

To

From

Date

Visit Christian Art Gifts, Inc., at www.christianartgifts.com.

Comforted by God: 100 Days of Healing and Hope for the Grief Journey

© 2024 by Boyd Bailey and Pat Elsberry. All rights reserved.

Published by Christian Art Gifts, Inc., Bloomingdale, IL, USA. In partnership with Kobus Johnsen of Johnsen, Inc.

First edition 2024.

Designed by Christian Art Gifts, Inc.

Cover and interior mages used under license from Shutterstock.com.

All Scripture quotations, unless otherwise indicated, are taken from the Holy Bible, New International Version®, NIV®. Copyright ©1973, 1978, 1984, 2011 by Biblica, Inc.™ Used by permission of Zondervan. All rights reserved worldwide.

Scripture quotations marked (AMP) are taken from the Amplified Bible, Copyright © 2015 by The Lockman Foundation. Used by permission. lockman.org

Scripture quotations marked (ESV) are taken from the ESV® Bible (The Holy Bible, English Standard Version®). © 2001 by Crossway, a publishing ministry of Good News Publishers. Used by permission. All rights reserved.

Scripture quotations marked (KJV) are from the King James Version of the Bible.

Scripture quotations marked (MSG) are taken from The Message, copyright © 1993, 2002, 2018 by Eugene H. Peterson. Used by permission of NavPress. All rights reserved. Represented by Tyndale House Publishers.

Scripture quotations marked (NASB) taken from the (NASB®) New American Standard Bible®, Copyright © 1960, 1971, 1977, 1995, 2020 by The Lockman Foundation. Used by permission. All rights reserved.

Scripture quotations marked (NKJV) are from the New King James Version®. Copyright © 1982 by Thomas Nelson. Used by permission. All rights reserved.

Scripture quotations marked (NLT) are taken from the Holy Bible, New Living Translation, copyright ©1996, 2004, 2015 by Tyndale House Foundation. Used by permission of Tyndale House Publishers, Carol Stream, Illinois 60188. All rights reserved.

Scripture quotations marked (TLB) are taken from The Living Bible, copyright © 1971 by Tyndale House Foundation. Used by permission of Tyndale House Publishers, Carol Stream, Illinois 60188. All rights reserved.

© All rights reserved. No part of this book may be reproduced in any form without permission in writing from the publisher, except in the case of brief quotations embodied in critical articles or reviews.

Most Christian Art titles may be purchased at bulk discounts by churches, non-profits, and corporations. For more information, please email SpecialMarkets@cagifts.com.

ISBN 978-1-63952-634-5

Printed in China.

29 28 27 26 25 24
10 9 8 7 6 5 4 3 2 1

Comforted by God

100 DAYS OF
HEALING AND HOPE
FOR THE GRIEF JOURNEY

PAT ELSBERRY
& BOYD BAILEY

Christian Art
PUBLISHERS

Introduction

Comforted by God is a devotional written to offer hope, healing, and encouragement to those who have experienced grief, loss, and trauma. Each message is authentically delivered as we address the myriad of emotions grievers face while walking through the grief journey. The book is written from our perspectives of what a person encounters as they go through the five stages of grief: denial, anger, bargaining, depression, and acceptance.

Although no one can escape death, and everyone will ultimately experience sorrow, it is a subject many are uncomfortable discussing. Yet, when *we* are in the throes of loss, we crave comfort and words of wisdom from those who have gone before us.

We have experienced grief firsthand, and throughout the pages we will openly share our hearts with each of you. Let's begin by giving you a small peek into our journeys.

Boyd's story

I am a former pastor who has experienced intense emotional pain after the divorce and death of my dad and mom and the grief of physical affliction in my battle with cancer. I am learning that abiding comfort is in God. Only God can heal my grieving heart. Only God can heal my excruciating hurt. Only God can heal my body. Only God can calm my country and community. Only God can make sense out of nonsense. Only God can take ashes and make something beautiful. Only God's unfailing love can bring comfort to my compounded sorrow. Only God. Only God. Mourning is medicine to bring me back to God. My laments are a language of love to my Lord, who hears with empathy and understanding.

"God blesses those who mourn,
for they will be comforted."

MATTHEW 5:4

Pat's story

I am a blogger, author, speaker, and passionate advocate for child loss, focusing on those who died from substance use disorder. My daughter was 38 years old when she died unexpectedly in 2020. While all loss is heartbreaking, child loss is an out-of-order death and a loss like no other. In 2021, I became a blogger, creating @HopeDuringLoss as an avenue to reach other parents who have experienced child loss and share with them the hope of Jesus during grief. As I moved forward in my journey, the Lord led me to write *Beautifully Broken: Finding Hope During Loss.* Just as I walked us through my journey with transparency and vulnerability in *Beautifully Broken* I carry you with me throughout the pages of *Comforted by God.* May the reliance on my faith touch you in a very real and palpable way as I give my heart a voice. My hope is to help others see that death is hard and the grief journey is one of the toughest roads we travel in life. Yet, living a life full of faithful trust is what brings us through the valley of the shadow of death.

As we walk through that valley, within the pages of *Comforted by God,* you will find the promise of hope when you walk this journey with Jesus by your side. Each message shines the light and love of Christ into the dark places where the sorrow and heartbreak now live. It doesn't camouflage the sorrow we experience with grief but instead will make you feel heard, witnessed, and understood when you are often in a place where you do not feel seen. Each message offers the comfort spoken of in 2 Corinthians 1:3-4.

"Praise be to the God and Father of our Lord Jesus Christ, the Father of compassion and the God of all comfort, who comforts us in all troubles so that we can comfort those in any trouble with the comfort we ourselves receive from God."

Love in Christ,

Boyd and Pat

Fellow Grievers

Acknowledgments

Grateful for friends and family who have comforted us with the comfort they received from God.

Dedication

To Melanie

01

Grief Journey

Whoever dwells in the shelter of the Most High will rest in the shadow of the Almighty. I will say of the Lord, "He is my refuge and my fortress, my God, in whom I trust."

PSALM 91:1-2

Our walk during the early days of grief seems to be the most arduous. We find ourselves barely limping along. Try as we might, sometimes the best we can do is get out of bed, take one breath at a time, and move our feet slowly, one in front of the other. If this is where you find yourself today, take heart, my fellow weary traveler. God understands these days. He not only walks beside us, but it's on these days when He carries us.

It was during one of the earliest days of walking this road when I made the decision that no matter what, I would follow Jesus. Was my heart broken? Yes. Was it going to be less broken if I walked away from my heavenly Father? Certainly not. Grief will be one of the hardest journeys we will travel, yet where else will we go? Who else can we run to? If we put our hope and trust in God, He will surely help us find our way.

"God is indeed my salvation;
I will trust and won't be afraid."

ISAIAH 12:3

Father, I need You today. Please cover me and lift me up when I feel as if I'm drowning. When I cannot take another step, please carry me through this darkest valley. I know that if I put my entire heart and soul into Your hands, Lord, I'll find the strength and peace I need for this journey. Please lead the way, Lord.

02

Grieving Process

"They will kill him [Jesus], and on the third day he will be raised to life." And the disciples were filled with grief.

MATTHEW 17:23

How are followers of Jesus to process severe sorrow? How do we keep on living when a child, parent, grandparent, or friend is now among the dead? Indeed, we let them down if we linger too long in despair, living as if there is no future hope after life. One way to honor the dead is to live well until we die. The loss of a loved one is a wake-up call that our existence on earth is finite. We are called by God to live purposefully for Him.

Ultimately, only Jesus can fill the void of human attachment. When deep-felt love is relocated to heaven, you need heaven's help. Grief is not to be processed alone, but with Almighty God and those who love you dearly. Open your hurting heart to genuine love, but do not succumb to a greedy or self-serving "friend" seeking to take advantage of your vulnerability. Guard your heart in your grief and give yourself fully to God.

"Our Savior, Christ Jesus ... has destroyed death and has brought life and immortality to light through the gospel."

2 TIMOTHY 1:10

Dear Lord, I lean into Your heart so my heart can grieve and be comforted by Your grace. Remind me that life is like a drop of water in time, but eternity with You is a sea of hope, healing, and happiness. Precious Lord, love me through my grief and lead me to those who are grieving so I can comfort others with Your words of life.

03

Where Is God in Grief?

The Lord is my rock, my fortress,
and my deliverer; my God is my rock.

PSALM 18:2

When I look back on the days before loss came knocking on my door, I both smile and cry. This is grief. It's a place where we can be both joyful and sorrowful at the same time. Our lives have been turned inside out, and we begin to wonder, *Where do we go from here? Is God even still here?* On the days when I look behind me, I stumble. On the days I look in front of me, I stumble. If I concentrate on the past or try to move toward the future there is heartache at every turn. What do I do? It's in these moments that I fall to my knees and cry out, "God, please help me."

Grief changes you. I don't believe I will ever be the same person I once was, but I'm still a person who believes. I'm confident that when I cry out to God, He is there for me. He promised never to leave me nor forsake me, and I trust His word to be true. After suffering a loss our hearts are shattered into a million little pieces. We wonder if we'll ever be whole again. Yet, when we are at our lowest, if we reach up and touch the hem of His garment, our healing will begin to take place.

"For our light and momentary troubles
are achieving for us an eternal glory."

2 CORINTHIANS 4:17

Lord, You know that my heart and my emotions are everywhere right now.

One moment I'm up, and the next moment I'm down. I am always missing my loved one, and some days I don't know how I'm going to survive the next hour. But I do know that You and Your Word are true and constant. No matter how I feel, I'm going to place my trust in You, Jesus. I commit my way to You.

04

A Refined Faith

In all this you greatly rejoice, though now for a little while you may have had to suffer grief in all kinds of trials. These have come so that the proven genuineness of your faith … may result in praise, glory, and honor when Jesus Christ is revealed.

1 PETER 1:6

Grief is a very real source of suffering. We grieve when we lose our loved one who has gone to be with the Lord. We may or may not totally get over their departure. The memory of the little things we shared in life could linger with us until the day we go to be with them in glory. We also grieve when we lose a child to foolish flings. We watch with broken hearts, as we are unable to control the harmful decisions of an adult son or daughter. We can suffer grief from all kinds of trials that create trouble. Yes, troubles are a test to refine our faith and to lead us to praise God.

Lean into the Lord's long-suffering and unconditional love as you grieve. Get to know your special friend Jesus at a new level. Enjoy solitude for a season, but avoid a prolonged trap of isolation. Engage with individuals and a care group who can grieve with you. Grief is not meant to be experienced alone. Processed pain is productive, but unprocessed pain is destructive. Rejoice, for though we suffer grief, we gain greater grace and deeper love from our heavenly Father.

"But you, God, see the trouble of the afflicted; you consider their grief and take it in hand."

PSALM 10:14

Heavenly Father, in my grief I receive Your greater grace and deeper love that brings healing to my heart. Give me the courage and faith to process my pain with other followers of Jesus so I can grow more like Jesus. Thank You, precious Lord, for seeing my trouble and afflictions and for holding me in the comfort of Your loving hand.

05

Comforted by Truth

"For my thoughts are not your thoughts, neither are your ways my ways," declares the Lord.

ISAIAH 55:8

When we are walking through the valley of the shadow of death, God can seem so far away. We often wonder, *Is God even real? Does He hear me? Does He see me?* From our limited perspective, we are met with silence, and now we feel abandoned and angry. *If God is real, how could He have let my loved one die?* These feelings of anger and hurt are normal. As we walk this earth, we are limited in our seeing and understanding. We may think back to the times we prayed and begged God to change the course of the path we found ourselves on. But what happened? Nothing. Or at least that's what our mere mortal minds tend to believe. Yet, as Christ's followers, if we pause for just a moment, we will remember that God is the Alpha and the Omega, the beginning and the end.

During the hard moments, we must hold fast to the truth that the things of Christ are a mystery to man. This is where *we walk by faith and not by sight.* Our heavenly Father loves us so much that He gave His only begotten Son for us. We may not understand the whys of today, but one day it will all be made clear. Our feelings are a normal part of the grief walk, and we mustn't berate ourselves for feeling them. God knows. It's during these times of anger and questioning when we should lean into the One who knows all.

"Praise be to the God and Father of our Lord Jesus Christ, the Father of compassion and the God of all comfort."

2 CORINTHIANS 1:3

Father, help me to hold on to You and our truths, especially during these times when don't understand Your plan. When I cannot see You or feel You, please remind me of Your Word and Your promises, in Jesus' mighty name.

06

Comforted by Mourning Well

Blessed are those who mourn,
for they will be comforted.

MATTHEW 5:4

Jesus instructs us to process our grief so we can be comforted. Sorrow is an everyday occurrence in this world, requiring a comfort that originates in Christ and is lived out by His Body—fellow followers of Jesus. The comfort of Christ through other Christians gives us permission to freely process our grief. Just as a soldier riddled with wounds and incapacitated requires the care of others, so a soul ravished by sorrow cannot heal itself without the comfort of love and kindness. If we resort to self-reliance or denial, we miss the soul care of grieving and remain in discomfort.

Cry out to Christ; He cries with you. He is your joy in life and your Comforter in death. Jesus is your hope in sickness and your strength in sorrow. The Lord is your peace in the storm and your living water during spiritual drought. God is your fortress of faith as you battle your fears, a refuge of acceptance when you suffer rejection. Christ is your life and the One who perfects His love within you. Mourn, be blessed, and be comforted. God loves you.

"If we love one another, God lives in us and his love is made complete in us."

1 JOHN 4:12

Heavenly Father, give me the grace
to process my grief and be comforted
by Your great love. Help me avoid
self-reliance and denial so I can
receive the medicine of grieving
and not live in discomfort. Show me
who I can share my fears and hurts with,
so I might be comforted and healed
by love's healing power.

07

A Heart with an Open Door

If anyone hears my voice and opens the door, I will come in and eat with that person, and they with me.

REVELATION 3:20

There are days when I cannot believe I'm here, walking this grief journey. How did I get here? I'm certain that at any moment I'm going to turn around and my daughter will be bounding through the door with that big, beautiful smile, saying, "Hey, Mama! What's for dinner?" As the days turn to weeks and weeks into months, I think perhaps she's just gone away on vacation, or she's living in another city. Surely this cannot be my life. Yet here I am, and I cry out, *Where are you, God? How could you let this happen?*

But when the unimaginable occurred and I wondered where God was, I remembered He isn't just a Bible character from days of old. He's my heavenly Father, and He knows what I am feeling. Even during the hurt, sadness, and missing of our loved one, we can hold on to His promise that during the hard times, He will never leave us. God isn't a God of yesterday. He is as real and present today as He was 2,000 years ago, even if we don't feel Him. My fellow grievers, I encourage you to open the door to your heart, even if just a crack. Jesus longs to hold us in His arms, wipe away our tears, calm our fears, and release the angst we feel. He longs for us to invite Him in, where we can crawl up into His lap and bare our hearts to Him.

"To comfort all who mourn, and provide for those who grieve ..."

ISAIAH 61:2-3

Father, You already know how I'm feeling without me saying a word. You know the deep sadness within my soul and the longing for my loved one. Please be the lifter of my head and heal my heart from this overwhelming sense of grief. Make Yourself known to me today, God, as I walk this road.

08

Grief's Conversion to Joy

Very truly I tell you, you will weep and mourn while the world rejoices. You will grieve, but your grief will turn to joy.

JOHN 16:20

Jesus prepared His disciples for the reality of grief—followed by His guarantee of joy. Jesus was going away, but He promised His followers He would see them again. What a comfort to know the eyes of the Lord are fixed on those He loves. The disciples would feel the pain of loss, but they could anticipate with joy Christ's return. The deep sorrow experienced at the foot of the cross would be surpassed by the height of joy standing at the empty tomb. Death brings sorrow, but life brings joy. We can smile and rejoice: our Suffering Servant has become our Living Lord!

What grief of yours needs a conversion to joy? You feel grief over a death, but you can trust that the Lord will bring joy back to your life. You feel pain over a prodigal child, but you can still pray for the return of joy to your heart—even if your child doesn't return. You feel disappointed over unmet expectations, but you can leave your desires in God's hands. He massages out the toxins of distrust so your joy is able to rehydrate your soul. You feel regret over a ruptured relationship, but you can seek the Lord's wisdom for relational repair as joy follows your repentance. Rejoicing will follow your mourning.

"They will come and shout for joy on the heights of Zion ... They will be like a well-watered garden, and they will sorrow no more."

JEREMIAH 31:12

Heavenly Father, in my grief I look to You for hope, healing, and peace. When I honestly express my sorrows, I know that You are the Man of Sorrows who transforms my pain into peace. I trust You with my pain so Your love and comfort can turn my sorrow into joy.

09

Sorrow Healed

God will wipe away every tear from their eyes.

REVELATION 7:17

We are all unique individuals. That's how God made us. Just like we all have different facial features and personalities, we all grieve differently. There are those who believe there is a certain time frame for grieving and a manner in which we should express our grief. This could not be further from the truth. There is no right or wrong way to grieve, and as much as we wish it were true, there is no fast track to getting through grief.

Each of us will walk our grief journey differently. The one thing we have in common is this: None of us can avoid grief. It's part of the circle of life, and not one of us can make it disappear or go away quickly. What we can do is be there for one another. Lifting each other up. Praying for one another. Speaking a kind word of encouragement. Offering a smile—a burst of hope where there may not be one. As difficult as your day might be, don't let the opportunity to positively touch someone else's life slip away. Walking this grief journey together can help us all begin to heal our brokenness … one day at a time.

"The Lord is my helper; I will not be afraid. What can mere mortals do to me?"

HEBREWS 13:6

Father God, thank You for making me who I am. I am Your child, and even though this grief journey may be the hardest walk I've taken, I want to walk every step with You. Provide opportunities where I may offer an encouraging word of support to another who is hurting. Although we are all different, we know that grief is grief and loss is loss. Our hearts all hurt the same, but You, Lord, are the healing balm that joins us together. In Jesus' mighty name, Amen.

IO

Sorrow from Not Following Jesus

"Come, take up the cross, and follow Me." But [the man] was sad at this word, and went away sorrowful, for he had great possessions.

MARK 10:21-22, NKJV

A disciplined, ambitious, intelligent, religious, and wealthy young man wanted to make sure he was in good standing with God, so he asked Jesus what he needed to do to gain eternal life. Jesus, in a loving response, asked the young man to give up what he loved most in order to love and follow Jesus. But the young man grieved, because he would gladly follow Jesus if he could follow him under one condition: that he could hold on to his earthly treasures and not be bothered with storing up treasure in heaven. The young man grieved because he did not want to exchange his gold for God.

When the Lord Jesus Christ fully possesses us, we don't possess anything. So when our house floods or burns down, we ask, "Lord, how can I help rebuild Your house?" When a child strays away from our love, we pray, "Lord show me how to love Your child." When a job goes away or a relationship walks away, we say, "Lord what is Your next season of service for me?" or "Help me let go and trust You with her." Grief over great possessions is comforted and healed when we give what we have to God and follow Jesus.

"For even if the mountains walk away and the hills fall to pieces, My love won't walk away from you, my covenant commitment of peace won't fall apart. The God who has compassion on you says so."

ISAIAH 54:10, MSG

Precious Jesus, help me let go of anything that is in the grip of my hands so I can embrace and hold Your love with both of my hands. Help me to obey Your words that lead me back to the healing path of joy. By faith, I seek first Your kingdom and trust You to provide for the necessities of life.

11

Being Your Authentic Self

The Lord is a refuge for the oppressed, a stronghold in times of trouble.

PSALM 9:9

Depression is the first cousin to grief. It's like the heaviest winter coat you could ever imagine wearing. After my daughter ran ahead to heaven, it was hard to manufacture feelings that weren't genuine. When I looked around and saw that everyone else's life was moving on, it hurt. How could everyone else be moving forward when my life was in a holding pattern? When reality sets in and we must begin facing the world, it's often unbearable. So, what do we do? We become a member of "The *Maskateers* Club." One of the ways grievers protect themselves to manage the myriad of emotions we experience is by wearing a mask.

We wear our masks not just for ourselves, but for others. We don't want to make those around us uncomfortable, so we smile on the outside even though we are crumbling on the inside. Although it's scary, we must remember that we are children of God, and He longs for us to be our authentic selves.

It is in our weakness that He is made strong. When we step out in faith, allowing ourselves to be transparent, we will then begin the healing process. Being vulnerable is hard, but it is also freeing. When we take the chance and remove our mask, letting others see who we really are, we are taking our first step toward healing our broken hearts.

"Be strong and courageous. Do not be afraid; do not be discouraged, for the Lord your God will be with you wherever you go."

JOSHUA 1:9

Father God, when I am feeling overwhelmed, remind me that You're here. Help me to remember that I can be my authentic self, the child You made me to be. Give me the courage to remove my mask in order to allow my heart to be healed by You. In Jesus' precious and mighty name, Amen.

12

Loving Patience out of Grief

"When the way is rough, your patience has a chance to grow ... For when your patience is finally in full bloom, then you will be ready for anything, strong in character, full and complete."

JAMES 1:3-4, TLB

James writes to a group of Jesus' followers, a minority culture of faith living among a majority people who persecuted Christians for their beliefs. These trials revealed the genuineness of their faith. Just as an exam exposes a student's true knowledge and understanding, so God's life tests reveal the reality of our relationship with Christ. A growing faith joyfully sees a problem as an opportunity to develop a more complete character and deepen our trust in God. The readers of James' letter were learning how patience could grow their capacity to persevere.

What grief are you experiencing that invites you into a patient faith? A financial loss? A relational death? Health challenges? An uncertain future? An unwanted change? By faith, seek to see your sorrow as hard but beautiful, difficult but determined, sad but glad in God. Wasted pain does not obtain a growing capacity for grace, but pain channeled into patience blooms into an exotic faith like the flower of paradise with the sweet taste of nectar. Even if a wound never heals or is not forgotten, you bow broken with an imperfect faith and rise perfected by a patient trust.

"We wait in hope for the Lord; he is our help and our shield. In him our hearts rejoice, for we trust in his holy name. May your unfailing love be with us, Lord, even as we put our hope in you."

PSALM 33:20-22

Heavenly Father, grow my patience so my hope is complete in You, through Christ's love. What loss am I experiencing that requires my steady patience, knowing that God is working out His plan? Lord, as I grieve my pain, grow my patience and empathy for others with hurting hearts.

13

Broken into Beautiful

To all who mourn in Israel, he will
give a crown of beauty for ashes,
a joyous blessing instead of mourning,
festive praise instead of despair.

ISAIAH 61:3, NLT

When grief strikes, *broken* is one of the first words that comes to mind to describe how we feel. Losing a loved one shatters our heart and mind, which can completely alter our lives. Grief changes us, and we may never be the same person we once were. But somehow, in the midst of the brokenness, when we put our trust in Jesus, He turns the broken into beautiful. It's like kintsugi, a Japanese art form where the areas of breakage in a piece of pottery are mended with lacquer, then dusted with powdered gold, silver, or platinum. This technique is derived from the words "kin," which means golden, and "tsugi," which means joinery. When translated, it means golden repair.

Kintsugi teaches us that broken places are not something to hide, but rather something to be displayed with pride. We may think we are broken and shattered beyond repair, but God sees something beautiful. If we surrender to Him, He will take our grief and sadness and turn our broken pieces into a thing of beauty and strength. Our pieces, once put back together, may be different than they once were. But just like a mosaic, we will see beauty once again. The cracks allow the light and the handiwork of our heavenly Father's loving hand to shine through.

"Cast your burden on the Lord [release it] and He will sustain and uphold you; He will never allow the righteous to be shaken (slip, fall, fail)."

PSALM 55:22, AMP

My precious Jesus, thank You for not being put off by my brokenness and the dark fragments of my life. Where I see irreparable hurt and brokenness, thank You for seeing beautiful. Thank You for restoring me piece by piece and helping me to believe again.

14

Repurposed to Serve

So here I [Caleb] am today, eighty-five years old! I am still as strong today as the day Moses sent me out … Now give me this hill country that the Lord promised me that day.

JOSHUA 14:10-12

With wholehearted devotion to the Lord, Caleb was a strong and fiery 85-year-old who challenged Joshua to give him the land they both had discovered and explored as young men. Joshua granted his friend's request and gave Caleb his inheritance. Instead of feeling angry over his loss or talking badly behind Joshua's back, Caleb boldly confronted his longtime friend with the truth of the Lord's promise. Instead of becoming a victim, he focused on his vision of God. Caleb kept his devotion to the Lord fresh so he could stay energized in serving others for God.

Enjoy the mountaintops and valleys of life, as each new season opens an unseen vista of the beauty of God's faithfulness and fruit from the orchard of your faithfulness. By God's grace, age elevates your perspective to see and appreciate people and things you may have ignored or been unaware of in the past. Relish these second-chance relational opportunities with your children or colleagues. As you move through loss to grace-based living, enjoy freedom's fun, but not at the expense of helping others find freedom through faith in Jesus. Repurpose for relational investments!

"For you have been called to live in freedom, my brothers and sisters. But don't use your freedom to satisfy your sinful nature. Instead, use your freedom to serve one another in love."

GALATIANS 5:13, NLT

Heavenly Father, as I move through seasons of loss, give me models of how to invest in and serve others with my time and money. Show me who needs me to intentionally invest in them with my experience and expertise. Reveal the beauty of Your fruitfulness out of faithfulness.

15

LOVED AND NOT ALONE

When doubts filled my mind, your comfort gave me renewed hope and cheer.

PSALM 94:19, NLT

On those challenging days when my heart is heavy and the tears are streaming down my face, I want nothing more than to crawl back into the safety of my bed and throw the covers over my head. I grow tired of the palpitations of my heart beating like a steel drum. Anxiety and fear have become the soul sisters I never knew I had. One day during my quiet time the Holy Spirit brought to mind the story of three Hebrew boys—Shadrach, Meshach, and Abednego. Because they wouldn't bow to the king's image, King Nebuchadnezzar had them thrown into the fiery furnace. He even had the guards heat it up seven times hotter! Instead of being anxiety-ridden and wringing their hands, what did they do? They began praising God. They put all their trust and hope in their heavenly Father, knowing that no matter what, God would protect and rescue them. Can you imagine the king's surprise when he peeked in and saw four figures walking around unharmed among the flames?

Most surprising of all, the fourth figure looked just like the Son of God. Imagine the faith and courage it must have taken for the three friends to even walk into the furnace. When life seems to be too much to bear and our instinct is to run in the other direction, we must remember there is Another in the fire with us. His name is Jesus, and He will never leave us.

"I prayed to the Lord, and he answered me. He freed me from all my fears."

PSALM 34:4, NLT

Father, on those days when I feel overwhelmed by all that is facing me, help me to remember that You are always walking beside me, ready to fight my battles and take me through the hard places.

16

One Person Pity Party

Elijah was afraid . . . and prayed that he might die. "I have had enough, Lord," he said.

1 KINGS 19:3-4

Great men and women of faith are not immune to severe insecurities. Elijah is calling down fire from heaven one day, and soon after is huddled, frightened, and depressed in a cold cave. Isolation feeds our insecurities. It is in our struggles that we need the prayers and support of God's people. Fear and grief have a way of backing you into a corner, making you feel trapped, and causing you to spiral down into a worst-case scenario. Maybe you have always been the one on the giving end, but now it's your opportunity to receive. You bless others when you accept their love. Look around and admit that you are the only attendee at your pity party, and humbly shut it down.

Lift your focus from yourself and your sorry situation and seek God. He has the grace you need to get through tough times—and your weakness is an opportunity for Christ's power to rest on you. Make sure mental, emotional, or physical fatigue has not flattened your faith. Get away and rest in the Lord. Take long walks and take in the wonders of Christ's creation. You may need to play before you can pray. Perhaps you need to engage a Christ-centered counselor to help you process your angst and anguish. Consider volunteering in service for Jesus, and your self-pity will transition into love for others. Pray away fear with love, asking, "How can I love my way out of my lamentations?"

"But he said to me, 'My grace is sufficient for you, for my power is made perfect in weakness.'"

2 CORINTHIANS 12:9

Heavenly Father, deliver me from self-pity to self-surrender to You and Your love. In what area of my life do I feel sorrow for myself, and how can I give that over to You and trust You with the outcomes? Help me to use my selfless service to Jesus to transform my self-pity into self-surrender.

17

One Day at a Time

Nevertheless, do not let this one fact escape your notice, beloved, that with the Lord one day is like a thousand years, and a thousand years is like one day.

2 PETER 3:8, AMP

Life can change in the blink of an eye. We've all heard the saying "what a difference a day makes," but when your loved one runs ahead to heaven, time takes on a whole different meaning. A year without them can seem just like yesterday and some days it can feel like a millennium. As we wander this ever-changing road of grief, we can be fine one moment, and in tears the next. Throughout it all, whether on the mountaintop or in the valley, God's peace and mercy are new every morning. In His all-encompassing love and compassion, He knows the ache of missing our loved ones.

God works in mysterious ways. He can shine light into the darkest places of our lives. Even the worst experiences will not destroy us—at least not forever. Tears and sadness are outward signs of all the love we will continue to carry in our hearts for our loved ones. As we see the days on the calendar go by, let us hold on, as it's yet another day closer to being in our true home—heaven—with our loved ones.

"It will happen in a moment, in the blink of an eye, when the last trumpet is blown. For when the trumpet sounds, those who have died will be raised to live forever. And we who are living will also be transformed."

1 CORINTHIANS 15:52, NLT

Father God, though You don't count time as I do, help me to keep my eyes on You, knowing one day all those who love You will be together again. Help me to remember that heaven is my home, and my loved one has just gone ahead before me. Until then, help me to keep my eyes fixed on You.

18

God's Ever-Present Love

There they are, overwhelmed with dread, for God is present in the company of the righteous.

PSALM 14:5

God is present in your predicament. You do not have to pray, "God, be with us." He is there already. He is there because He cares. He is there because you are extremely valuable to Him. God cherishes His children. He loves to give His own good gifts (Matthew 7:11). His presence alone is a present. He is present to give wisdom. He is present to give you directions. He is present to give you courage. In His presence there is peace. God's presence is there to calm and convict us. His peace is what propels us forward by faith. You are not alone!

Do not give up on doing the right thing. Sinful compromise for short-term satisfaction never ends well. Why put your family at risk by running after forbidden fruit? God has not left you. He does not wink at wicked deeds. He is right by your side to see you through every sinful temptation. In the middle of your hard times, seek hard after your heavenly Father in solitude and prayer. His presence invites you into intimacy. Design your life around a daily retreat into His presence. Look into His face and feel His love. In His presence, He provides just what we need for each moment. In your pain, persevere in prayer without ceasing. Healing comes in God's presence.

"God is our refuge and strength, an ever-present help in trouble."

PSALM 46:1

Dear Lord, I praise You for Your ever-present love for me to lean on. Lead me to another who loves You, whom I can ask to pray for me to rest in Your love. Help me to design my life around a daily retreat into Your presence, and to moment by moment throughout the day rest in You.

19

The Right Release

Love is patient and kind; love does not envy or boast; it is not arrogant or rude. It does not insist on its own way; it is not irritable or resentful.

1 CORINTHIANS 13:4-5, ESV

There is a myth that surrounds grievers. Some say you need to let go of your loved one. But it's not letting go of our loved ones that will heal our hearts. Rather, we need to learn to let go of the pain, anger, and fear that plague us after loss. When someone dies, all of our love doesn't disappear. It remains. We will continue to love them until we are joined together again one day. Letting go of the sadness, anger, hurt, guilt, and anxiety will help us focus on all the joy and goodness our loved ones brought to our lives.

The common misconception of "time heals all wounds" couldn't be further from the truth. Even though time is different in heaven than here on earth, time isn't what heals us—God is. Grief has become my magnifying glass and has allowed me to see more clearly than ever before. It's like a person who has had cataract surgery. Before surgery, your vision is cloudy and dull. Once the bandage is removed, you see all you were missing.

Colors are more vivid, and objects are so much sharper. Leaning into the arms of Jesus not only helps make things clear, but it also helps lessen the pain of the missing piece of our heart as we remember the love more than the loss.

"The Lord is close to the brokenhearted and saves those who are crushed in spirit."

PSALM 34:18

Lord Jesus, it's unfortunate that we must go through loss to see things differently, but I'm ever grateful that You make all things new. By walking this grief journey with You by my side, I am better able to love and support others who are also hurting.

20

Praise Brings Peace

Praise the Lord. Blessed are those who fear the Lord, who find great delight in his commands.

PSALM 112:1

Praising the Lord and fear of the Lord help shift our focus from sorrow to comforting peace. This is the heart of a child of God in love with and loyal to his or her heavenly Father. The worship of Jesus causes the eyes of faith to see Him in His glory. His great love secures the soul, and His hallowed holiness pierces the heart, resulting in joy and reverence for God. When Christ is the core of our belief system, the natural outcome is peace, joy, and happiness. Jesus gives His children His promises so we can walk by faith, trusting that He will do what He said He would do.

Praise positions a hurting heart to be in the healing presence of Jesus Christ. It is in the presence of Jesus that joy wells up in our inner being. Circumstances and menacing threats cannot take away the joy of the Lord. We bow our heads in fear of the Lord and then lift our eyes toward heaven in worship. What is the secret to happiness in this life? It is holding with an open hand the temporal and grasping with a firm hand of faith the eternal. It is maintaining an unwavering focus on God and not being disillusioned by other well-meaning—or not so well-meaning—Christians. If your joy is gone, comfort your sorrows with praise to the Lord. Praise brings peace.

"Whatever you have learned or received or heard from me, or seen in me—put it into practice. And the God of peace will be with you."

PHILIPPIANS 4:9

Heavenly Father, I worship You in the glory of Your holiness, I bless You and praise You for being God Almighty. Lord, help me find happiness in what brings You happiness. Remind me to lift my eyes and heart to You in grateful praise and to delight in Your commands.

21

Sharing Our Wonderful Terrible Truth

The Lord is good, a stronghold in the day of trouble; he knows those who take refuge in him.

NAHUM 1:7, ESV

There are many faces of grief. We've all experienced that awkward moment when you run into someone, and they ask, "how are you?" This is followed by a pregnant pause while you wonder if you should answer honestly or just say, "I'm fine" and move on. Over time, I've found my best answer is, "I'm doing fine today," emphasizing the word *today.* Not everyone wants to hear how we are feeling, and it's also not necessary for us to share our deep feelings with every person who comes our way. However, it may make us feel better to share our truth without oversharing.

When asked how she was doing, Kay Warren, who lost her son to suicide several years ago, always replies, "wonderful–terrible." She explained how she truly has a blessed life and has many days where she feels wonderful. But underneath it all, there will always be some terrible because her child has died. Regardless of how much time goes by, there is a hole in our hearts where our loved one belongs that no one else can fill. Grief has many faces, and they are not all met with a downturned smile. There will always be sadness, but grief also shares the face of determination, faith, trust, and hope. Layering these faces on top of the faces of sorrow and heartbreak may provide a realistic look at how grief is every day.

"You are my hiding place and my shield; I hope in your word."

PSALM 119:114, ESV

Father, thank You for lifting me up and walking with me on all of my wonderful-terrible days. I'm so grateful I can count on You to be with me and walk with me in both the sunshine and the rain.

22

Humbled by Health Issues

So, he went down and dipped himself in the Jordan seven times, as the man of God had told him, and his flesh was restored and became clean like that of a young boy.

2 KINGS 5:14

Softening happens when sickness seizes the body. There is a sensitivity and tenderness of heart that may have been dormant in the behavior of a Christian. But a body under fire from illness makes us let go of control and cling to Christ. At first, there may be an angry reaction, then we succumb to a sense that God's got it—He is in control. Faith in the face of fiery trials is the fruit of humility. Sickness is an invitation to submit to Jesus and lean into His healing love.

Yes, there are acts of obedience that accompany a life smothered by a cloud of uncertainty. As we walk in humility, we listen for the Lord's voice. He speaks through His Word, His teachers, His preachers, His children, and experts in treating physical ailments. Prayer and modern medicine are a powerful partnership in producing positive outcomes. A humbled heart creates clarity of mind for wise decision-making. Allow the Lord to use health issues to bring vulnerability and intimacy into your relationships. Be real about your fears and ill feelings, and allow friends to comfort you. Emotional awareness and engagement are healthy outcomes of a humbled heart. Renew your mind with Scripture and bend your will toward God. A humbled heart hears the Lord.

"Lord, do not forsake me; do not be far from me, my God. Come quickly to help me, my Lord and my Savior."

PSALM 38:21-22

Heavenly Father, I humble my heart so I can hear from You and be healed. Show me how to channel my suffering from sickness in a way that draws me deeper in my love for Jesus and others. Lord, use health issues to bring vulnerability and intimacy into my relationship with You and others.

23

Knocked Down, but Not Knocked Out

The Lord himself will fight for you. Just stay calm.

EXODUS 14:14, NLT

Many people compare walking the grief journey to the rhythm of ocean waves. Oftentimes I've felt more like a boxer in the middle of the ring. Life can be moving along in a forward fashion, when out of nowhere, there is a trigger: a song, a smell, a memory, or a date on the calendar. It's an unexpected blow, like a sucker punch to the gut, and once again, we are knocked off our feet. We are reminded that we are fighting a giant. It may be one you can't see with your eyes, but can certainly feel deep within your soul. Who is this contender? His name is Grief.

When we find ourselves back in the ring, our senses become heightened, and we're left standing there, waiting for the next blow. But take heart; there is hope during loss. One day we will wake up feeling stronger, ready to fight for our lives. Just like when a boxer perseveres to the end to claim his victory, we can look toward the One who can help us endure. We can't fight this battle on our own, but we don't have to! We are not in this fight alone. So, what do we do? We look at the contender in front of us and realize he is nothing compared to the giant inside us! We might be knocked down, but we are not knocked out. The giant inside of us is the Holy Spirit. His might and the power of God's Word will carry us through.

"For I am the Lord your God who takes hold of your right hand and says to you, Do not fear; I will help you."

ISAIAH 41:13

Father, I'm ever so grateful for the gift of Your Holy Spirit. We are powerless by ourselves, but we are more than conquerors through You, who love us. Thank You for carrying me in the palm of Your strong and mighty hand.

24

Fight Club

But you, man of God, flee from all this, and pursue righteousness, godliness, faith, love, endurance, and gentleness. Fight the good fight of the faith. Take hold of the eternal life.

1 TIMOTHY 6:11-12

Paul reminds Timothy to run from the rancid fruit of love of money—selfishness, self-reliance, and self-perseverance—and rather pursue the eternal values of righteousness, godliness, faith, love, endurance, and gentleness. Paul nudged Timothy away from passive autonomy to an active community. He encouraged him to make his good confession in the presence of many witnesses. Paul knew his protégé needed people in his life to protect him from himself and to help him battle unbelief. Joining a community of Christ's followers gives us courage and clarity to carry on in our battle to believe.

Most of all, remember God has already won the war. The Lord Almighty is the greatest tactician of life's battles, and He equips you with trust when you feel defeated, fills you with forgiveness when you feel angry, marshals your courage when fear stalks your soul, and guards your vulnerable, loving heart with the peace of Christ. Stay in the good fight of the faith.

There will be bruises that need bandages, but Jesus heals the brokenhearted and binds up their wounds. Only those who fail to fight lose—so fight in love, as love eventually wins over all enemies.

"Yet I will show love to Judah; and I will save them—not by bow, sword or battle, or by horses and horsemen, but I, the Lord their God, will save them."

HOSEA 1:7

Dear Lord, humble my heart to engage other Jesus followers to help me overcome life's battles. Show me a community of Christ followers with whom I can do life together, through its ups and downs. Sharpen my most effective weapon of love with Your love.

25

Healing My Heart: Step by Small Step

And the peace of God, which transcends all understanding, will guard your hearts and your minds in Christ Jesus.

PHILIPPIANS 4:7

A few years ago, I found myself walking a path no one ever dreams of taking—the grief journey due to child loss. Although death is part of the circle of life, child loss, an out-of-order death, is particularly heartbreaking. When my daughter ran ahead to heaven unexpectedly, my heart was broken in a way I had never imagined it could be. Yet God, in all His magnificence and wonder, immediately covered me in a way that could only be described as miraculous. I still had days when I wept uncontrollably, but I continued to feel His presence on those dark days. It was like a shield surrounding and protecting me.

When our loved ones move to heaven, no matter how much we may try, there is no rushing through the grief journey. And there is no going around it. Instead, we must walk through it and let our heavenly Father heal our hearts, step by small step. What an incredible comfort to know we are genuinely never really alone.

If you have found yourself walking this grief journey, be kind and gentle with yourself. Lean into the One who made you. God is walking alongside us, and when we need it, He will carry us through the valley of the shadow of death.

"I'll never let you down, never walk off and leave you."

HEBREWS 13:5, MSG

Lord, help me to remember that I am never truly alone. Even on my darkest night, You are with me and are close like no other. You know what it means to grieve, and You are healing my heart, step by small step. Thank You for surrounding me and comforting me with Your peace that truly does surpass my earthly understanding.

26

Preemptive Physical Care

Give us nothing but vegetables to eat and water to drink … At the end of the ten days they looked healthier and better nourished than any of the young men who ate the royal food.

DANIEL 1:12, 15

There is physical stewardship required of every soul saved by Jesus Christ. In the same sensitive way the spirit of a person is cared for, their body also needs proper attention. As age increases with time, physical health requires intentionality. Yes, some are called to physically suffer for Christ's sake, but the Lord does not want His children to ignorantly neglect their health. Bodies need intentional care. Like Daniel, be different from the crowd and surround yourself with friends who have the conviction to eat right and exercise. Gluttony limits your influence for the Lord. A disciplined lifestyle leans into a routine of allowing past your lips only groceries untainted from man's toxic preservatives. Your body stays fresh when it is nourished by fresh foods. Slow down, plan healthy meals, and feel better. You are wise not to wait for disease to attack before you change.

It is easier to take wise measures now, before it's too late. So schedule your annual physical, write out your menu for the week, increase your grocery budget, eat out less, and learn to see your health as a stewardship. Jesus expects you to love Him with your body and soul!

"And thou shalt love the Lord thy God with all thy heart, and with all thy soul, and with all thy mind, and with all thy strength: this is the first commandment."

MARK 12:30, KJV

Lord, how would You have me take care of the body You have given me for Your glory? Show me how to channel my sufferings in a way that draws me deeper into my love for You and others. Help me to embrace and celebrate healthy habits.

27

LEARNING FROM GRIEF

There is a time for everything, and a season for every activity under the heavens: a time to be born and a time to die.

ECCLESIASTES 3:1-2

As a student of sorrow, I'm learning as I go. I don't think we ever get over our grief; we learn how to live around it. There is a time and season for everything, including a time to grieve. Just because our loved one died doesn't mean that our love died with them. God promises to heal our broken hearts, but it takes time. As He heals our brokenness, we learn how to live with joy and sorrow. Healing from grief is not about moving on, but moving forward.

One of my most significant learnings is realizing that grief is love—it's all our love for our loved ones with no place to go. As we heal from grief, we learn how to acknowledge our loss and create space for it. When we're progressing through our grief, we learn how to love the one who ran ahead to heaven with the same deep joy and passion we had for them when they were alive. The grief isn't as all-consuming and intense as it may have once been. Grief isn't one-size-fits-all. There is no time limit, and we must walk our own path, moving forward as we can. As we walk, let us always remember we are never walking alone.

"So do not fear, for I am with you; do not be dismayed, for I am your God. I will strengthen you and help you; I will uphold you with my righteous right hand."

ISAIAH 41:10

Lord, during those times I am an unwilling student in this grief class, thank You for being the ultimate Teacher. Knowing that You love me with an everlasting love helps me move forward.

28

Shadow of Death

Even though I walk through the darkest valley,
I will fear no evil, for you are with me;
your rod and your staff, they comfort me.

PSALM 23:4

Everyone walks through life in the long shadow of death. There are those who try to delay death's effects with surgery, medicine, diet, and exercise, but all of us eventually die. Death for the dying can be a shadow of discomfort, discouragement, and even despair. It is in death's valley that faith is tested, families are stressed, and friends rally in prayer. How do you serve someone who is in their last months or days on earth? First, you live before them a life of faith. A dying loved one needs love from those who know the Lord so that they can know the Lord.

We all walk toward death, but in Christ, it is a passage to eternal life. It's hard when a believing parent begins to lose their ability to think clearly, but we patiently listen to their irrational words, knowing that one day they will speak with the tongues of angels. Our faith in Jesus triumphs over death, and it also comforts us on the way to death. The destination of this life is death, but, when traveling with the Lord, there is no need to fear evil or the unknown. His presence is all we need to persevere in righteous living. Hope, peace, and love are an outflow of walking with Jesus through the lonely valley of death. Thanks be to God, who gives us victory over death in Christ!

"'Where, O death, is your victory?
Where, O death, is your sting?' . . .
But thanks be to God! He gives us the
victory through our Lord Jesus Christ."

1 CORINTHIANS 15:55-57

Dear Lord, I need You to walk with me through the valleys and up the mountains so my soul rests in You and is restored by Your love. Give me the grace to serve a dying loved one who needs love from those who know the Lord, so that they can come to know Your sweet love and forgiveness.

29

Healing and Restoration

To all who mourn in Israel, he will give a crown of beauty for ashes.

ISAIAH 61:3, NLT

When you suffer a loss, and the grief is deep, healing and restoration can seem far off and unattainable. Yet God is a God of healing and deliverance. We don't just wake up one day with our hearts totally healed and restored. He restores us piece by piece, day by day. This grief journey reminds me of a time when my mother-in-law gifted my husband and me with two pieces of antique furniture that had been in their family for over 130 years. It was a sweet gesture, but when we saw their condition, we couldn't imagine them in our brand-new home. Although each piece had beautiful stained, leaded glass in the doors, the wood hadn't been adequately cared for in years and had a covering of dark black lacquer. We didn't want to offend her, so we took them home, where they found a place in our garage.

After a few months, we decided to try and restore the pieces ourselves. We spent our free time with steel wool in hand, cleaning, stripping, and scrubbing. Just about when I was ready to give up, I noticed beautiful tiger oak wood in excellent condition just below the thick black covering. That was our incentive to continue moving forward. Imagine what God can do for His children if we can take a piece of furniture that is dark and ugly and turn it into a thing of beauty. He longs to remove the heavy darkness that has settled over our broken hearts and bring restoration and healing to us.

"Come to me, all you who are weary and burdened, and I will give you rest."

MATTHEW 11:28

Jesus, thank You for taking the dark, broken pieces of my heart and restoring them to a thing of beauty.

30

Thankful for Answered Prayer

Then Jesus looked up and said, "Father, I thank you that you have heard me. I knew that you always hear me, but I said this for the benefit of the people standing here, that they may believe that you sent me."

JOHN 11:41-42

Jesus thanked His Father for answering His prayer before the prayer was answered. His heart was so in tune with the heart of the Father that He could boldly ask, knowing it was the will of God. In the same way, our Savior calls us to align our hearts with our heavenly Father's heart. His plan is for our desires to be His desires, our wants to be His wants, our goals to be His goals, our will to be His will, and our prayers to be His prayers. We ask in Christ's name when our desire is for our answered prayers to be a benefit for believers to grow in their faith and for unbelievers to come to faith.

What prayers are yet to be answered, but need to be prayed? What is Christ asking you to confidently pray in His name, knowing He will answer in the future? Perhaps it's a yet-to-be-determined job promotion you can thank God for now. You can praise the Lord today for your wayward child, whom you have peace in your heart will eventually come back to his Savior Jesus. Or, you pray with the Spirit's certainty over an uncertain illness that threatens your joy. Whatever you face, you can face down with faith in your heavenly Father who hears your prayer.

"You may ask me for anything in my name, and I will do it."

JOHN 14:14

Heavenly Father, I praise You for the assurance of answered prayers in the future, and I thank You for prayers You have already lovingly answered. Whatever I face in life, Lord, I trust You, the One who hears my prayers and who leads me in love and obedience while I wait on Your best.

31

Permission to Grieve

And now these three remain: faith, hope and love. But the greatest of these is love.

1 CORINTHIANS 13:13

While there are hundreds of grief quotes to draw from, there is one that sums it up best: "Grief is the price we pay for love." This well-known quote by Queen Elizabeth II is a gift to those who are grieving—the gift of agreement. It's like being given permission to grieve for the loss of your loved one, as it is just another way to express all the love you have stored up in your heart with no place to go. Have you had well-meaning family or friends tell you it's time to move on? After some time has passed, expectations are frequently thrust upon us. One of the most common is that *enough time* has gone by, and we should *be over* our grief. Let me simply say there is no time limit for grieving. Grief is the price we pay for love.

The grief journey is a tricky road to navigate, but on those days when our hearts are heavy, viewing our grief from the perspective of love may help lift our spirits heavenward. While we continue to move forward in life, we can experience grief and joy simultaneously. Our love for those who have run ahead to heaven doesn't fade away but remains forever. Let us move forward with loving kindness, leaning into Jesus, the one true rock and strength of our lives.

"I love you, Lord, my strength. The Lord is my rock, my fortress, and my deliverer; my God is my rock, in whom I take refuge, my shield and the horn of my salvation, my stronghold … The Lord lives! Praise be to my Rock! Exalted be God my Savior!"

PSALM 18:1-2, 46

Jesus, Your name is above all names, and You are worthy to be praised. I am so grateful to call You Father, Friend, Deliverer, and the solid Rock of my salvation.

32

What Do You Want Jesus to Do?

Jesus stopped and ordered the man to be brought to him. When he came near, Jesus asked him, "What do you want me to do for you?"

LUKE 18:40-41

What do you want me to do for you? The generous, kind words of Jesus went right to the heart of the hurting man. The wailing blind beggar had asked Jesus to have pity on him. But Jesus went beyond feeling sorry for the man's pitiful situation and instead offered him a blank check. Wow! Wisely the man asked for healing of body and soul—and immediately, his faith became a catalyst of Christ's healing—100 percent and forever. No more groping about in fear. No more being mocked for being a blind beggar. At that moment, the man knew what he needed Jesus to do—fully heal him!

What do you need Jesus to do for you? You may need Him to meet you in the quiet stillness of His intimate love. Ponder the loving deeds of the Lord in your life. Be hilariously grateful! Wisdom comes from seeking the perspective of Providence—the One who knows all and is able to show you what you need to know. So listen and learn from the Lord. Keep the faith, even if you are not sure of the next step. The Holy Spirit will direct your path. Invite Jesus to do for you what you cannot do for yourself—bring clarity and comfort. Trust His ways so that they become yours. Let Jesus do what only He can do for you!

"Let the one who is wise heed these things and ponder the loving deeds of the Lord."

PSALM 107:43

Heavenly Father, I need You to lead me by Your love and wisdom. Show me what I need You to do for me—that I cannot do for myself. When I weep over a loss, I trust You to wipe away my tears and comfort my hurting heart. And when I rejoice, I praise You for rejoicing with me.

33

The Healer of Broken Hearts

For we live by faith, not by sight.

2 CORINTHIANS 5:7

No matter how many days, months, or years go by, there will always be a piece of my heart that will remain on this never-ending grief journey. Yet, in the midst of the grief, I'm so grateful there is also a Healer of Broken Hearts. His name is Jesus, and we walk this journey side-by-side. During the early days of grief, I didn't think I'd be able to survive. But God in all His magnificence has covered, comforted, and carried me when I didn't think I would make it another day. He is the healer of broken hearts. Though we may not understand all the reasons for the journey we find ourselves on, we know who can turn it all around. Only God can make beauty from ashes.

Someone once asked if I believed our hearts could be healed after suffering loss. I absolutely do. I've been standing on God's promise that He will be "close to the brokenhearted" and save "those who are crushed in spirit" (Psalm 34:18). Granted, it takes time, along with a lot of grief work, which might entail professional help, medication, prayer, and many other things. While time may not heal all wounds, time does lessen the overwhelming, sharp, tsunami-like feelings early grief brings. If you're hurting today and missing your loved one, I encourage you to hold on. God will do as He has promised. Don't give up. Keep running to the Father. He will never let you down.

"The steadfast love of the Lord never ceases; his mercies never come to an end; they are new every morning; great is your faithfulness."

LAMENTATIONS 3:22-23, ESV

Lord Jesus, thank You for being the healer of my heart and the lifter of my head. On those days when I am feeling especially overwhelmed by the loss of my loved one, thank You for Your love and faithfulness. Thank You for pulling me up out of the pit of despair and setting my feet on sturdy ground.

34

Hold On to Hope

Let us hold unswervingly to the hope we profess, for he who promised is faithful.

HEBREWS 10:23

Faith creates hope, so where faith is conceived, hope is birthed. Yes, hope is the daughter of faith. Those who profess to know Jesus as their Lord and Savior possess hope. Hard times try to hinder hope's comforting company, but it is unhindered whenever faith in God is the focus. Those who hold on to hope are at peace. Where faith peers, hope makes clear. Where there is a wall, hope finds a door. Where there is darkness, hope looks for light. Hope expects Christ to come through. Hope is confidence in Jesus Christ, period. It is confidence that He is faithful to follow through with His promise to provide peace in the middle of our turmoil.

When hope is deferred, avoid rejecting God and giving up. Wait on the Lord and hope in Him. He helps you when you feel helpless. He empowers you when you feel powerless. He encourages you when you feel discouraged. He gives joy when you feel joyless. He gives life and a reason to live. Hope never disappoints. If you let go of hope, your gracious Lord doesn't let go of you. Like Mount Everest, your hope is unmovable, so hold unswervingly to your living hope: Jesus.

"I wait for the Lord, my whole being waits, and in his word I put my hope."

PSALM 130:5

Heavenly Father, help me to hope in You when all seems hopeless. Show me in what situation I need to hope for the best and plan for the worst. I praise You that Your hope is unmovable, and I hold unswervingly to Your living hope: Jesus Christ.

35

Speaking Life into Our Brokenness

The tongue has the power of life and death.

PROVERBS 18:21

Isn't it amazing how one of the smallest parts of our body is both the strongest and the deadliest? Some may think the most vital part of the body is the heart or lungs. While those certainly are significant organs that give us life and strength, they are not the parts I'm referring to. The smallest and most potent part of the body is the tongue. Do you realize that our words can either speak life or speak death? Our tongues and the words that so easily roll off of them can help build others up or they can tear them down. A few simple words can destroy a life, a friendship, or a family. The power of the tongue and the words we say do not just impact others. The words we speak about ourselves can have life-altering repercussions.

Perhaps you've heard the old adage, "out of the heart, the mouth speaks." What you think and say about yourself can breathe life and death into existence. When life's circumstances have got you feeling down, it's easy to say things like, "I'm so depressed. I'm so sick. I hate this life. I don't want to live anymore. I give up!" My friend, these are words of death you're speaking over yourself. The next time you feel down, raise your head a little higher and look up. Even if you don't feel it, speak it out loud and into your heart. Speak life into your dry bones and watch them awaken. You matter. You are loved. You have favor with God and man. You are strong.

"The soothing tongue is a tree of life,
but a perverse tongue crushes the spirit."

PROVERBS 15:4

Lord, thank You for loving us even when we may not feel lovable. No matter what, thank You for breathing life, hope, and love into our hearts and minds. Thank You for making us more than conquerors.

36

Love Nurtures Healthy Emotions

Love the Lord your God with all your heart.

MARK 12:30

People who are emotionally healthy understand their flaws and accept their imperfections as they rely on God's grace and forgiveness. Because they know themselves and have experienced God's forgiveness, they are able to extend grace and forgiveness to others. Emotionally healthy individuals take captive their thoughts, understand their feelings, and control their behavior. When facing life's challenges, they become better, not bitter. They learn to process pain so it does not fester into ongoing relational conflict. The emotionally healthy love God and are loved by God, so they are able to love for God. They are peaceful people.

Jesus starts at the heart of the matter—our heart. The heart is the seat of our feelings and affections. What captures our passions and yearnings? We are drawn to what we desire—what we value. And the heart follows what it treasures above all else. In the same way an engaged couple each aggressively seeks to engage the heart of their lover, so as the bride of

Christ, we passionately pursue His heart. As our heart loves Jesus, He simultaneously settles and stirs our emotions.

"A good man brings good things out of the good stored up in his heart, and an evil man brings evil things out of the evil stored up in his heart. For the mouth speaks what the heart is full of."

LUKE 6:45

Heavenly Father, I submit to Your Spirit and ask You to be the manager and filter of my emotions. Show me who needs me to be more honest with my emotions in a loving manner. Help me make love the most powerful weapon in my arsenal of faith and, like the tip of an arrow, may it point others to You.

37

Small but Powerful

For now we see only a reflection as in a mirror; then we shall see face to face. Now I know in part; then I shall know fully, even as I am fully known.

1 CORINTHIANS 13:12

WHY. The word is made up of three small letters, but it holds a powerful punch. If you've lost a loved one and find yourself on the grief journey, I wouldn't be surprised if you've asked yourself this 3-letter word. It probably has gone something like this: *Why did this happen? Why did my loved one have to die? Why didn't things turn out differently? God, why didn't you intervene and stop this bad thing from happening? Why? Why? Why?* We've all been there, and although we often won't find an answer this side of heaven, there is another question we could ask ourselves that may help. It's not why, but who.

Who's your Daddy? As Christ's followers, if we are confident that God is our heavenly Father, then we know who our Daddy is. When we were children, we trusted in our parents and all they told us, even when we didn't understand their reasoning. When challenges come our way and death knocks on our door, we may not understand, but placing our total trust in Jesus, and knowing it will all be revealed to us one day, can alleviate some of the anger and hurt that accompanies grief.

"Trust in the Lord with all your heart
and lean not on your own understanding;
in all your ways submit to him, and he
will make your paths straight."

PROVERBS 3:5-6

Father God, thank You for being my Daddy. Even when I may not understand why You've allowed certain things to happen in my life, my trust remains in You. No matter what happens, Lord, my hope and faith will forever remain in You.

38

Stilled and Quieted

But I have calmed and quieted myself,
I am like a weaned child with its mother;
like a weaned child I am content.

PSALM 131:2

The raging waves of the world's worries crash against the shore of our souls. At work, it may be missed deadlines or mismanagement of money. At home, it may be miscommunication or a monster of a problem with one of our children. At school, it may be the misconduct of others or the misfortune of feeling alone. Life is loud, and sometimes its deafening tones tune out our trust in God.

Only in silence can our soul be resuscitated by our Savior Jesus. He works wonders when we wait before Him. We are clamorous without Christ, but in the presence of His grace, our soul is subdued and soothed. Calm and contentment come forth by faith when we are stilled and quieted before Christ. We are like a child basking in the love of a devoted parent. A mother is a comfort to her weaned child, since she is no longer merely a source of sustenance. They have a true relationship. As you linger quietly with the Lord in anticipation, He may not give you what you want—but He will give you what you need. You may want to leave, but He knows you need to stay. You may want to get, but He knows you need to give. By God's grace, remain childlike in your faith and character. Keep your heart humble and honest under heaven's hope. As a child looks to his mother for comfort and security, look to your Savior Jesus for His quiet confidence and strength. A heart kept by Christ lives for Christ. Settle your soul in stillness and solitude with Jesus.

"As a mother comforts her child,
so will I comfort you; and you will
be comforted over Jerusalem."

ISAIAH 66:13

Heavenly Father, still my soul and quiet my spirit by Your Holy Spirit so I might rest in Your comfort, as a child is comforted by her mother. Slow me down to be loved by the countenance of Your care and the light of Your wisdom. I choose to rest in Your grace and walk in Your truth.

39

The Healing Power of Tears

Jesus wept.

JOHN 11:35

I was raised to never air our dirty laundry in public and to always smile and keep a stiff upper lip. Do those phrases sound familiar to you? When someone we love dies, it's often hard to "fake it until you make it." I spent years perfecting my mask-wearing, but when someone we love dies, it's hard to carry on as though everything is fine and normal. One day I was reminded about the shortest verse in the Bible: Jesus wept. I realized that if Jesus could cry, surely I can too!

During those moments when grief is biting at our heels and not letting up, remember that it's OK to not be OK. Washington Irving said, "Tears speak more eloquently than ten thousand tongues. They are the messengers of overwhelming grief, of deep contrition, and of unspeakable love." So instead of bottling all of that up inside you, feel free to remove your mask and let it flow. There may be a time and place for being strong and stoic, but it's not now. Be your authentic self and let your truth be told. Let your heart feel free to express all that is within, and don't hold anything back.

"You keep track of all my sorrows.
You have collected all my tears in
your bottle. You have recorded
each one in your book."

PSALM 56:8, NLT

Oh, Father, thank You for making me with a heart that can weep when it feels sad and lonely. Thank You for collecting all my tears. As each one falls, You cleanse my spirit from its heaviness. You alone are the one who lifts me up when I am down and carries me when I can no longer walk. Thank You for continuing to heal my heart.

40

JOYFUL OR RESENTFUL

The older brother became angry and refused to go in. So his father went out and pleaded with him.

LUKE 15:28

The elder son in Jesus' famous parable of the prodigal cannot get beyond his feelings of neglect. He isn't honored for being a compliant child all his days, and instead, his father throws a feast for his wayward brother. This lack of attention from his "insensitive dad" boils into anger as he watches his lascivious brother enjoy the unconditional love of their father. A motivation of loving and joyful obedience had been replaced by a drive for rigid rule-keeping rooted in pride. When the fear of being left out turns into reality, resentment rushes in to protest and squash all joy.

Has resentment robbed your joy? Are you able to celebrate another's good fortune in the face of your misfortune? One way to better understand your heart is to ask others if you are a complainer and blamer or are grateful. Do you take responsibility for your actions? Immaturity obsesses over the splinter in a colleague's eye and seeks to deny or dismiss the plank of pride that skews its own perspective. Mature followers of Jesus, on the other hand, rejoice when a friend's foolish choices lead him back home to the Father's love. Joy celebrates a life enjoying God's blessing.

"Do not remember the rebellious sins of my youth. Remember me in the light of your unfailing love, for you are merciful, O Lord."

PSALM 25:7, NLT

Loving Father, I celebrate Your generous grace and mercy to me and desire to extend it to others. Show me whom I can celebrate with, and remind me that any hint of resentment is relationally draining. Help me to remember that Your joy energizes my life, work, and relationships.

41

How a Mess Can Become Your Message

I have told you these things, so that in me you may have peace. In this world you will have trouble. But take heart! I have overcome the world.

JOHN 16:33

Have you ever wondered why your life has unfolded like it has or asked yourself, *Why me?* Do you feel as if your life is a hot mess? Or maybe you looked around, and everyone seemed to be living their best life—except you. I'm not suggesting we have a pity party, but these are all typical questions and feelings when we walk through challenging times. We all go through periods when life is hard, such as when we're grieving the loss of a loved one, suffer a job loss, or receive a diagnosis that pulls the rug out from under our feet. Friend, if you can hold on for a little bit longer, what you consider a mess now may one day become your message.

Someone once told me I had a black cloud hanging over my head. Interestingly, from my perspective, I didn't think so. It's called life, and it was just a hard season. I don't know the circumstances you're facing, but we serve a good God, even during the trials and turmoil of life. Every cloud, even the black ones, has a silver lining. If you're struggling and wondering *why me*, I encourage you to lean into God. He can and will turn your mess into a message for Him. He will use your story to reach someone else who is hurting. He isn't finished with you yet!

"For I consider that the sufferings of this present time are not worth comparing with the glory that is to be revealed to us."

ROMANS 8:18, ESV

Father, thank You for the reminder that You never promised us a carefree life. I am so grateful I have placed my whole heart and trust in You. Thank You for turning my mess into a message that shines a light on Your goodness.

42

Less of Me

Have this mind among yourselves, which is yours in Christ Jesus, who, though he was in the form of God, did not count equality with God a thing to be grasped, but emptied himself, by taking the form of a servant.

PHILIPPIANS 2:5-7, ESV

To be born was Jesus' supreme act of emptying Himself. He emptied Himself by trading heaven's perfection for earth's imperfections. He emptied Himself by going from reigning with the Trinity from all eternity to serving for 33 years in a temporal world, so all could see God in the flesh. He emptied Himself of life so that through His death and resurrection, all who believe could find life on earth and for eternity. Jesus modeled "less of me" by humbling Himself in obedience to His heavenly Father's will for His life. Perfect love led Him to assume the body of a perfect life.

Less of me and more of the Lord. Less of my agenda and more of God's will for my life. Less of my demands and more humble requests that Christ fill me with His love so that I can support my spouse in his dreams and desires. Less of my needs being met and more attentiveness to my neighbor's needs: a walk to hear her hurting heart or a meal together to celebrate her new opportunity at work. Less of me so I can be more available and attentive to my grandchildren and children, so they can know who they are and who they want to become, so they know how special and loved they are by their heavenly Father and by me. For Love's sake, I give up my life to give life!

"Whoever wants to become great among you must be your servant."

MATTHEW 20:26

Precious Lord, lead me to empty myself and fill me with Your Spirit. Show me how to spend less time thinking of myself and more time thinking of others. By faith, I empty myself so the Spirit can fill me and reveal how I can best love others so they can become the best version of themselves.

43

Forgiveness: The Sixth Stage of Grief

Be kind and compassionate to one another, forgiving each other, just as in Christ God forgave you.

EPHESIANS 4:32

Much has been written about the five stages of grief: Denial, Anger, Bargaining, Depression, and Acceptance. As if this were not enough to deal with as we grieve, I think we could add one more stage to the list—Forgiveness for ourselves and our loved ones. When a loved one dies unexpectedly, your mind begins to feel like the inside of a tornadic wind tunnel where myriad questions swirl around rapidly. What could I have done differently? How could I have stopped this? How did I miss the signs?

As we grieve, we often have a weight of heaviness that is not seen or felt by others. It's like carrying a backpack full of heavy river rocks each day. Since we cannot rewrite history and those questions can haunt us, forgiving ourselves and our loved ones is the first step to healing. Perhaps your loved one did some things that caused you to harbor anger and unforgiveness in your heart. Or maybe you're simply angry because they died and left you. What a gift we have in Jesus. We can run to Him asking for forgiveness, and as we let go of everything we hold on to, we open the door to peace. As we seek forgiveness, it will be like removing the rocks from our backpack, one at a time. We will eventually feel lighter, and a peace we may have never known existed will begin to permeate our hearts and minds.

"You, Lord, are forgiving and good, abounding in love to all who call to you."

PSALM 86:5

Heavenly Father, how merciful and gracious You are to never turn Your back on us. Thank You for forgiving me and letting me release any hurt and anger I've been holding in my heart. Thank You for replacing these feelings with Your peace and everlasting love.

44

Contemplation for Change

May these words of my mouth and this meditation of my heart be pleasing in your sight, Lord, my Rock and my Redeemer.

PSALM 19:14

This phrase in Psalm 19 is a prayer, a benediction that keeps us centered on what matters most—the Lord, our Rock, and our Redeemer. Our words are a reflection of our hearts, so we make sure to meditate in our hearts on what matters most—thoughts, words, and actions that please the Lord. Words stirred in grace display luscious art on the canvas of life. Every word is a unique color and creation that either brings attention to the Creator or conspires with enemies of the faith: the world, the flesh, and the devil. Love focuses on the faithful Rock, a generous Redeemer.

By faith, embrace the fact that contemplation saves you time. Your prayers are a sacrifice of praise to God, who graciously receives and gives back to you in the form of blessings: The blessing of being healthy. The blessing that the necessities of life are more than taken care of. The blessing of children who want to be with you and who want to serve others. The blessing of work. The blessing of rest. The blessing of being loved and being able to love others well. Contemplate Christ so that you can be changed. Ask Him how He loves you. Pause, listen, and do likewise.

"O God, we meditate on your unfailing love."

PSALM 48:9

Heavenly Father, I praise You for Your unfailing love; help me to love others as You love me. Show me what life rhythms I need to change so that You can change me through contemplation of Your love for me. I contemplate on You so You become greater and I grow in humility.

45

Self Care Is Not Selfish

Come to Me, all you who labor and are heavy laden, and I will give you rest. Take My yoke upon you and learn from Me, for I am gentle and lowly in heart, and you will find rest for your souls. For My yoke is easy and My burden is light.

MATTHEW 11:28-30, NKJV

It's been said that you cannot draw from an empty vessel. Truer words have never been spoken. No matter your specific story, if you're on this grief journey, you will surely feel broken and beaten up by life at some point. You can look at the grief chart and understand that you will go through each step of the grief cycle. But it can be frustrating when you realize you can end up going through some of the same steps over and over again. You think you're doing so well, and wham! Out of nowhere, you're back underwater again.

When you feel empty and overburdened, it's time to step back and take some time to fill yourself up. Self-care is not selfish. Even Jesus took time away after ministering to the needs of others. How many times did He leave the disciples to go off alone to pray? Just like Jesus, we need to spend time with our heavenly Father and fill ourselves back up. This may mean different things to different people, but whether that's an early morning walk, a spa treatment, a quiet time of prayer and reflection, a good long cry, or a cup of your favorite coffee shared with a friend, do it. Whatever self-care means to you, fill yourself up and love yourself in the best way you can.

"God is within her, she will not fall;
God will help her at break of day."

PSALM 46:5

Heavenly Father, how great is Your love for us. When we run into Your arms or fall at Your feet, You are there to lift us up and renew our hearts and spirits so we can get back up again. Thank You for a love that endures forever.

46

Love a Hurting Friend

*Therefore, my brothers and sisters,
you whom I love and long for, my
joy and crown, stand firm in the
Lord in this way, dear friends!*

PHILIPPIANS 4:1

Paul writes to those whom God led him to invest time, truth, and love to, so that they might grow closer to Christ in faith and love. The joy of watching friends grow in faith brought the deepest soul satisfaction to Paul. These friends had stuck with him and had remained faithful to the Lord through the years. Since he loved them, Paul longed to be with them. Life's crowning achievement for this famous apostle was loving others well. Love looks for ways to be together.

What friend can you honor by making time to be with them? A life that rushes from one relationship to another dizzies the soul and preempts expressing true feelings. This relational malpractice carries the costly penalty of misunderstandings and unmet expectations. Fortunately, those of us who walk with Jesus learn from the Lord how to walk with friends in humility and love. Remember, some friends look up to you to point them to Christ's love, while other friends show you the love of Christ. Be with both. Be with the younger ones to pay forward the generous love already invested in you, and be with older friends for them to enjoy the fruit of their love for you. Love and long for beloved friends!

"For this reason, ever since I heard about your faith in the Lord Jesus and your love for all God's people, I have not stopped giving thanks for you, remembering you in my prayers."

EPHESIANS 1:15-16

Heavenly Father, I praise and thank You for friends who point me to You. I love to love them and be with them. Lead me to younger and older friends that long to be with me. Help me to love with understanding and in ways that are helpful and bring healing and life.

47

Grieving with Hope

Blessed be the God and Father of our Lord Jesus Christ! According to his great mercy, he has caused us to be born again to a living hope through the resurrection of Jesus Christ from the dead.

1 PETER 1:3, ESV

The first time I ever heard the term "grieving with hope," I was only days into the grief journey. I'd never heard this expression before and discovered it is derived from Scripture: "And now, dear brothers and sisters, we want you to know what will happen to the believers who have died so you will not grieve like people who have no hope"(1 Thessalonians 4:13, NLT). As soon as I could wrap my broken heart and mind around this Scripture, I clung to it like my personal life preserver.

Though I'm grateful for this promise, the reality is that there will still be grief while we are on this side of heaven. No matter who you are, you will encounter grief, pain, and sadness at some point in your life. Even as Christians, the death of someone we love is excruciating. It's not because we are afraid for them; it's because of the empty place they have left behind in our hearts. Healing unfolds in its own time frame. It doesn't look at a watch or a calendar to determine a specific timing. But as you encounter the waves of grief, I hope you will also reach out and grab hold of this life preserver before you. May you grieve with hope, knowing this is not the end.

"So with you: Now is your time of grief,
but I will see you again and you will rejoice,
and no one will take away your joy."

JOHN 16:22

Heavenly Father, we are forever grateful for the sacrifice Your Son, Jesus, made on the cross for us. It is because of this sacrifice that we can grieve with the hope of seeing our loved ones again one day.

48

Love Grows by Obedience

But those who obey God's word truly
show how completely they love him.
That is how we know we are living in him.
Those who say they live in God
should live their lives as Jesus did.

1 JOHN 2:5-6, NLT

John reminds us that the cross of Christ is not just a one-time belief of salvation but an ongoing working out of our salvation in love. The cross is a commandant of love to be lived out as Jesus lived and loved. It is the daily practice of dying to our selfish desires and coming alive to selfless service. Jesus is the Word of Truth to be embraced and obeyed. Our imitation of Christ is His invitation to intimate love. Our total trust and obedience show how completely we love Jesus. When we first believed, we only began to fathom the depths of God's love—revealed over time.

Is your love being made complete by your obedience to Christ's commands? Your next level of loving better may mean forgiving an unfair critic, apologizing to a coworker, serving the poor, respecting someone who doesn't deserve respect, or deferring to what a friend or family member wants. Love grows as a motivation when obedience moves from duty to delight. Surrender to *His will be done* and release *my will be done.* Begin to stretch your soul by being still and warming up your spirit with Scripture reflection and listening in prayer to what the Spirit is saying. Once you experience perfect love, then truly obey by loving others as you have been loved.

"Dear children, let's not merely say that we love each other; let us show the truth by our actions."

1 JOHN 3:18, NLT

Heavenly Father, show me how much You love me so that I can love and obey You. Lead me to those who need my love, forgiveness, and comfort to help heal their hurting heart. I praise You that the cross is a commandant of love to be lived out as Jesus lived and loved.

49

Compartmentalizing Grief

Be strong and courageous. Do not be afraid; do not be discouraged, for the Lord your God will be with you wherever you go.

JOSHUA 1:9

While we can be so grateful God continues to heal our broken hearts, there are times when the heaviness and brokenness is still there if we dare to look deep within. It's churning away like slow-burning embers after a horrific fire. While the flames have been put out, significant damage has been done because the loss and destruction remain underneath. One of the ways we may deal with the loss is by placing parts of our grief in little compartments in our minds. It's like a waffle. We may only want to deal with what's in one waffle square before we jump to another. While we need to do the necessary grief work in order to heal, sometimes compartmentalizing our sorrow isn't such a bad thing. At specific points on this journey, it's a form of self-preservation.

It may seem disenchanting to realize that these feelings of grief continue to crop up even years later, but in reality, it just makes us human. Grief is never one-and-done. When you're ready, take a moment and look at the road behind you. Notice all the terrain you've covered and be proud of how far you've come! All the large boulders and potholes encountered in the early days, when you could barely climb out or around them, are behind you. If you find you're compartmentalizing your grief, it's OK. No matter where you are on this journey, give yourself credit for every step it took to get here. It's all progress … one step, one moment, one breath at a time.

"But to each one of us grace has been given as Christ apportioned it."

EPHESIANS 4:7

Heavenly Father, thank You for continuing to pour out Your love, Your grace, and Your strength upon me so that I may be all that You want me to be. Help me to see how far I've come instead of how far I've yet to go.

50

Wounded for Another

This is my command: Love one another the way I [Jesus] loved you. This is the very best way to love. Put your life on the line for your friends.

JOHN 15:13, MSG

Wounds are not for the faint of heart. One wintery day, I forgot to grab my work gloves before I moved some firewood. You guessed it—halfway through my project, my finger grazed the side of a sliver of wood barely protruding and, like a sharp syringe, it made its way into my exposed flesh. The pain was sudden, then gone, but within minutes the pierced skin puffed up red and began to pulsate with pain. I tried to push through, but soon I relented; the pain needed attention. I stopped and found my daughter Rachel for assistance. Having done "splinter surgery" multiple times with her three children, it was no sweat for her to help dad. She dug and twisted and, within a few minutes, extracted the intruder.

Wounds are like this—accidents, not intentional. When a friend bears my burden of emotional hurt by hurting with me, my healing begins. When I go to my best friend Jesus and say out loud my unfulfilled longings, He enters into my pain with loving patience and helps me better align my desires with His. My wounded healer has healing in His wings for me if I choose to rest in the shadow of His loving presence. Jesus was willing to be wounded so healing can come to all who come to Him in repentance and faith. Is another wounded? Offer healing love. Are you wounded? Let love heal your heart. Love heals.

"But God demonstrates his own love for us in this: While we were still sinners, Christ died for us."

ROMANS 5:8

Heavenly Father, help me be willing to be wounded to help another be healed. Lead me to the person who needs me to step up and help bear her burden. Help me to be brave, willing, and generous to be wounded so that another can be healed.

51

Anxiety + Fear = Grief

*Let the peace of Christ rule in your hearts,
since as members of one body you were
called to peace. And be thankful.*

COLOSSIANS 3:15

Grief is not typically synonymous with peace, yet as we ache for comfort after losing a loved one, we need peace as much as we need air to breathe. As our lives come to a screeching halt after the death of a loved one, we are often met with anxiety and fear. Maybe you're waiting for the other shoe to drop and are afraid something will happen to another family member. Take heart, dear one, you are not alone.

Like a wolf in sheep's clothing, who knew that grief comes disguised as fear? Anxiety and fear are among the most common ways grief affects those who are walking this journey. Stop where you are. Take a deep breath and know these are normal responses to life's hardest traumas. You aren't crazy! You are human, and you're doing great! You're walking through the valley of the shadow of death, fighting your way forward. Press on, and rest assured that you are not walking this journey by yourself. God is there with us every step, even when we don't feel him. When we worry in the middle of the night, He is our courage. He is our strength when we don't think we are strong enough to win this fight. Trust Jesus and lay all your fears at His feet. This act of faith will bring peace and calm to your spirit like nothing else can.

"So do not fear, for I am with you; do not be dismayed, for I am your God. I will strengthen you and help you; I will uphold you with my righteous right hand."

ISAIAH 41:10

Precious Heavenly Father, thank You for being the peace within my storm. When fear and anxiety begin to grip my heart, please be the peace that surrounds me. Thank You for bringing calm to my spirit and all that surrounds me.

52

Healing Isolation's Pain

A man with leprosy came to Jesus, imploring Him and kneeling down, and saying to Him, "If You are willing, You can make me clean." Moved with compassion, Jesus reached out with His hand and touched him, and said to him, "I am willing; be cleansed."

MARK 1:40-41, NASB

My friend who lives two states north of me shared how his younger brother was close to death. He was heartbroken; his grieving had already commenced. "He is the kindest man I have ever met—I'm so grateful my brother is ready to see the loving face of Jesus." My friend's brother was a COVID victim, connected to the hissing ventilator—like a venomous snake, sucking the life from his once-vibrant body. Isolated. Dark. In danger. Alone and afraid. But hopeful, as heaven waited to greet him. This kind of death is so hard. Yet God's love heals isolation's pain.

Jesus encountered the sad sight of a precious man who was inflicted with incurable leprosy—quarantined for a lifetime of isolation. He was saddled with the shameful task of declaring himself unclean to anyone who might venture too close—as if seeing his wretched condition was not warning enough. But his desperate situation caused his tortured soul to seek out the only One who could free his mind and body from the prison of pain. Hopeful, he implored his Creator to make right this wrong—and Jesus, as He was so often, was moved with compassion to touch the untouchable. Compassion cleansed him. The inoculation to isolation's pain is to first totally trust the loving touch of Jesus.

"Wait for God, for I will again praise Him
for the help of His presence, my God."

PSALM 42:5, NASB

Heavenly Father, help me to lean into Your healing compassion to heal my pain. I bring my body to You as a living sacrifice, holy and acceptable for You to heal, as is Your will. Inoculate me from isolation's pain with Your loving presence and with the comforting community of believers.

53

Anger: The Silence of Grief

Refrain from anger and turn from wrath;
do not fret—it leads only to evil.

PSALM 37:8

When grieving a loved one, it's pretty typical to question God and even turn away from Him. Our silence toward Him is exhibited in a variety of ways. Have you found yourself angry with God for letting your loved one die? How often have you shared some words with God that weren't so pretty? Really, anger is grief that has been silent for too long. We can stifle our anger about our loss for only so long; it will eventually come bubbling up to the surface. And just like a volcano's hot lava, it will erupt right before our eyes, burning and scorching everything and everyone in its path.

Instead of seething underneath, share your anger, hurt, and questions with God. It's okay to yell, scream, and cry. The deadly silence of grief and undercurrent of rage hurt the most. We can say anything we want to God. He has big shoulders, and He can handle our emotions. If we let the anger grow and steep within, we are limiting how the Holy Spirit can move. It's like slowly turning off the power to the one thing that can keep you moving in the right direction. When anger fuels grief, it becomes eerily quiet deep within. Grief's silence then becomes quite deafening. Maybe you're wrestling with something in your heart today. If you are, I'm sorry you're struggling. The fastest way to get settled and back on track is to run to the Father. Thankfully, even when we are upset with him, He never turns His back on us.

"The Lord is near to all who call on him."

PSALM 145:18

Dear God, You are a most loving and compassionate Father. I'm so grateful that even when I am angry with You, You never turn Your back on me. Thank You for loving me through it all, especially the hard parts.

54

Moving from Sad to Glad

Always be full of joy in the Lord. I say it again—rejoice! Let everyone see that you are considerate in all you do. Remember, the Lord is coming soon. Don't worry about anything; instead, pray about everything. Tell God what you need, and thank him for all he has done.

PHILIPPIANS 4:4-6, NLT

The apostle Paul knew sad circumstances firsthand: he experienced chronic physical limitations (his thorn in the flesh), rejection from political and religious authorities, and time in prison. Yet, drawing on his own experiences, he reminds other followers of Jesus who are sad in spirit to focus our hope in the Lord—because He is coming soon. Paul then tells us to release our worries, and instead pray about everything. How? "Tell God what you need, and thank him for all he has done." The Lord God has a track record of faithfulness that is 100 percent trustworthy. His love converts sadness to gladness.

How do you move from being sad to being glad? Recognize the reality of grief. God created you to grieve. Without a healthy process of mourning your loss, you will miss the comfort of

Christ and His followers and be stuck in a cycle of pain, anger, and discomfort. Humble yourself before the Lord and choose words to describe your broken heart: *Lord, I am mad, I miss her, I am ashamed, I hurt, I feel alone; help me to have hope in You. Restore the joy of my salvation.* And, once you have been generously loved by perfect love, make sure to be empathetic toward those struggling to smile. Love them as God loves you. Mourn together so that you can rejoice together.

"Will you not revive us again, that your people may rejoice in you?"

PSALM 85:6

Heavenly Father, in the world, I am sad, but in You, I am glad. Help me to rest in you. Lead me to a friend I can confide in, who knows and loves You, whom I can tell of my sorrows and ask for her comfort and prayers. As I receive generous comfort, help me to generously comfort others.

55

Where Are You, God?

Turn to me and be gracious to me, for I am lonely and afflicted. Relieve the troubles of my heart and free me from my anguish.

PSALM 25:16-17

We will all experience losing a loved one at some point. Death summons the most profound emotions and can make the strongest believer question their faith. Have you ever found yourself asking, *Where are you, God?* This is a typical question during grief, but one with no easy answer. It's not like God will pop up, waving His hands and shouting, "Here I am! I'm sitting by this fig tree, waiting to chat with you." If only it worked like that. But God is here. He is as close to us as the air we breathe. We just need to call out His name. He hears us and will be right there, walking alongside us.

While loss can be devastating, it helps to focus on three key areas: Trust, Faith, and Hope. Fixing our eyes on these things will help us navigate the difficult parts of life's journey. When we do, we can trust that God is who He says He is. We can have faith that His Word is true, and we can hold on to the hope of Christ. When you are wondering where God is, remember that He will fill your tank when you're empty. He will lift you up and carry you when you cannot take one more step. And He knows your heartache and will heal your crushed spirit. The journey through grief isn't one of instant gratification, but something we have to work at every single day.

"Those who know your name trust in you, for you, Lord, have never forsaken those who seek you."

PSALM 9:10

Father God, when I'm so overwhelmed and wondering where You are, help me to remember all the times You have been there for me. If I can remember only one word, let it be this: Jesus—my strong tower and the name above all names.

56

Go Public with Your Pain and Be Healed

Therefore confess your sins to each other and pray for each other so that you may be healed. The prayer of a righteous person is powerful and effective.

JAMES 5:16

I am learning that if I *conceal* my problems, they will become a big deal. But if I *reveal* my problems, there is a high probability I will be healed. For example, in my marriage, my wife Rita and I are learning to share our differences with another mature couple or Christian counselor to help us move from being relationally and emotionally stuck. Maybe anger has caused emotional distance in our hearts. We still love each other, but at times we find it hard to like each other. Revealing this to another person we trust keeps us from concealing pain that is spiraling toward resentment.

Some introverts may find it harder to share their feelings. To wrap words around wounds. You are private, and you feel like you are the only one dealing with personal problems. The heart of the matter may be that you don't even like yourself. You are deceived and believe that your faults are unique to you, so pride is keeping you from being honest about your deep hurts. The pain of revealing problems has not yet exceeded the pain of concealing problems. In the meantime, it eats away at your energy; anger is the emotional undercurrent. Humility asks for help. If you humble yourself by revealing your hurts, you will take the first step in repairing relationships and healing your heart. Doing nothing is not an option for a humble heart. Silent sufferers need another to bear their burdens and, in the process, they will be healed by Christ's love.

"Carry each other's burdens, and in this way you will fulfill the law of Christ."

GALATIANS 6:2

Heavenly Father, give me the courage to reveal my problems so that I can be healed. Lead me to people with whom I can share my troubles with a humble and teachable heart. Give me the courage to reveal my hurt to another I trust, to free me from concealed pain so I can be healed.

57

The Anchor

This hope is a strong and trustworthy anchor for our souls. It leads us through the curtain into God's inner sanctuary.

HEBREWS 6:19, NLT

While vacationing by the water, it's always nice to watch the beautiful boats go by. Whether a lovely sailboat or a stunning yacht, each one is lovely in its own right. But have you ever taken time to look at the anchor? Probably not. The anchor isn't easily visible, but if you think about it, it is one of the most critical parts of any boat. Anchors are generally massive and appear sturdy and heavy looking. This vast unbreakable piece of iron is attached to a long rope or chain. When the boat's captain gets ready to settle in for the night, he feels confident that as he throws the anchor overboard, it will do what it is intended to do.

But what would happen if the rope wasn't strong enough and broke free from the anchor? The anchor would become entrenched in the bottom of the ocean, and the boat would be left adrift. The anchor and the rope are just like us and our relationship with Jesus. As we walk this grief journey, having Jesus as our anchor will make the road we traverse so much smoother. He's the one thing that keeps us afloat during the stormy days of grief. When Jesus ascended to heaven, He promised to send us His Spirit to be our Helper and Comforter. So if Jesus is our anchor, then the Holy Spirit is our rope. To be our best and most secure in life, we must have both.

"But the fact of the matter is that it is best for you that I go away, for if I don't, the Comforter won't come. If I do, he will—for I will send him to you."

JOHN 16:7, TLB

Jesus, when I'm tired from fighting the heaviness of grief, thank You for being my anchor and strengthening me. Thank You for the gift of the Holy Spirit, the rope that keeps me safely tethered to You.

58

Sick of Being Sorrowful

Jesus said, "This sickness will not end in death. No, it is for God's glory so that God's Son may be glorified through it."

JOHN 11:4

Are you struggling with sorrow? If so, seek to experience the intimacy of God's glory in the middle of your grief. Your afflictions can be eclipsed by His glory. Similar to the stamina of a mother caring for a needy child, His glory engulfs your soul with the energy to endure chronic pain. The Spirit provides security in your heartache. Christ's peace guards your heart and mind. God's glory gives you hope and healing. The Lord uses sorrow and mourning to draw people to each other and to Himself. A sick child causes Mom and Dad to come together on their knees on behalf of their precious one. Elderly parents provide the opportunity for adult children to spend time together and to work together for the betterment of their parent's quality of life. Grief can be a blessing.

Is someone you love suffering from an illness? How can you glorify God in your love for them? Start with a simple prayer for the Holy Spirit to strengthen your sick friend with His grace and love. Share Scriptures such as Psalm 59:16-17 to give them comfort and peace. Your faith in God is a rock to those whose world is being rocked by adversity. Be available to support them by caring for their children or raising funds to pay for their medical bills. When we are prepared to give a reason for our hope in Him, God's people love and serve like Jesus, glorifying Him.

"The spirit of a man sustains him in sickness, but as for a broken spirit, who can bear it?"

PROVERBS 18:14, AMP

Heavenly Father, use my illness or the sickness of a loved one to bring glory to my Savior, Jesus Christ. I trust You for the time and resources to care for a loved one's chronic illness. Dear Lord, use my faith in You as a restoring refuge to those whose world is being rocked by adversity.

59

The Dance of Grief

Joy is gone from our hearts;
our dancing has turned to mourning.

LAMENTATIONS 5:15

Whenever I think about dancing, I remember happy times, like dancing with my husband at our wedding. Or the fun times as a teenager attending the Friday night dances at our church. But did you ever equate dancing with grief? While watching an awards show, I was mesmerized by one artist's incredible dance routine. Each move and footstep seemed to be carefully choreographed when suddenly, as he glided along smoothly, he jumped into the air and came crashing to the floor. His body began moving in jerking motions, leaving me perplexed.

His dance moves were very much like the dance of grief. We are up one minute, gliding along smoothly, when all of a sudden, in the next moment, we find ourselves upside down in a heap on the floor. While we are grateful for the smooth, easygoing times, there are days when we are left twirling around on our heads like breakdancers. And just like dancing, this grief journey has many different rhythms. Oh, how we wish for a regular cadence instead of a booming staccato one moment and a quiet interlude of waterscapes the next. Yet grief has its own timetable. There is no set schedule, and although we are told there are stages to grief, it's important to realize we may visit some stages more than once. It doesn't mean anything is wrong with us; this is the dance of grief. It's essential to allow ourselves to feel what we feel. It's part of the healing process.

"You have turned for me my mourning into dancing; You have put off my sackcloth and girded me with gladness, To the end that my glory may sing praise to You and not be silent. O Lord my God, I will give thanks to You forever."

PSALM 30:11-12, NKJV

Father, thank You for being Lord over all things—the joyful and the sorrowful. My trust remains in You. Give me the energy to dance with You and allow You to lead even when my feet of faith fumble along, hurting and unsure.

60

Mountaintops and Valleys

He [Jesus] climbed the mountain to pray, taking Peter, John, and James along. While he was in prayer, the appearance of his face changed and his clothes became blinding white. At once two men were there talking with him. They turned out to be Moses and Elijah—and what a glorious appearance they made!

LUKE 9:28-30, MSG

Mercy and love kiss the cheeks of faith when we are experiencing the mountaintops of life. The vistas of God's faithfulness are fully exposed: past, present, and future. What He has done, what He is doing, and what He will do. Perspective. Ah, sweet perspective. Mountaintops are necessary to inspire and equip us for the valleys. Indeed, most of life is experienced in the valleys. Many of our everyday encounters at work and home are mundane and misshapen. Our spirit longs to remain on the mountaintop, but our calling from Christ is to follow Him and love others through the valleys.

Mountaintops are meant to transform you by the glory of God, and valleys are designed to conform you to be more like

Christ by the grace of God. Like Jesus, be intentional with your prayer time so you can be in the presence of love and mercy. But remember, remaining on the mountaintop in a perpetual state of solitude and spiritual ecstasy is not permanent, but preparation. Getting dirty in the valley of death, suffering, and sin is your calling. Cherish the mountaintops for giving you the perspective to be effective for God in the valleys.

"God, my shepherd! I don't need a thing.
You have bedded me down in lush meadows,
you find me quiet pools to drink from.
True to your word, you let me catch my
breath and send me in the right direction."

PSALM 23:1-3, MSG

Heavenly Father, keep me focused on You during the good times and during the difficult days. Give me Your perspective during the mountaintops so I can serve You well in the valleys. Use mountaintops to transform me by Your glory and valleys to conform me to be more like Jesus.

61

Sympathy vs. Understanding

"Remember your word to your servant, for you have given me hope. My comfort in my suffering is this: Your promise preserves my life."

PSALM 119:49-50

When it comes to grief and loss, what do you think is most important—to have sympathy or understanding? *Sympathy* is a feeling of sincere concern for someone experiencing something difficult or painful. On the other hand, *understanding* is having knowledge about a subject or a situation. When my daughter first ran ahead to heaven, during those early hours and days, there was a wave of phone calls, texts, emails, and people coming to our home. We were flooded with sympathy, shown in both word and deed. I will be forever grateful for those who lifted me up in many ways. There is no way to repay that kind of love and care, which is precisely what was needed during those early days.

Then as time moved forward, I found that my needs began to change. I began to seek out those who had understanding. I didn't want to feel pitied. Even though people meant well, I grew weary of hearing the words, "I'm so sorry." So which is more important to have—sympathy or understanding? Really, we need both. We just need them at different times. As we mourn our loved ones, there comes a moment when there is a turning point, and our needs shift. We are drawn to those who have understanding, the ones who know firsthand the pain of losing someone they love. Sympathy gets us through those hard, unbearable early days. Understanding is what helps sustain and rebuild our broken hearts.

"Great is our Lord and mighty in power;
his understanding has no limit."

PSALM 147:5

God, thank You for those who offered genuine sympathy when I needed it during those challenging early days. I'm so grateful You also brought others to walk alongside me who could uplift me and provide understanding when I was ready for that part of the journey. You are my Almighty Father and know what I need and when to offer it.

62

Trials Resulting from Our Choices

The Lord gave this message to Jonah son of Amittai: "Get up and go to the great city of Nineveh ..." But Jonah got up and went in the opposite direction.

JONAH 1:1-3, NLT

Jonah disobeyed the Lord's call to call out the wicked behavior in Nineveh. He ran away from the Lord and thought he could hide on a ship. When we run away from God, we may feel like we are getting away with something because the consequences of disobedience are not always immediate. But as sure as the rising of the sun burns away the darkness and shrinks back shadows, so the light of God's love reveals distorted loves. When we choose to turn our back on the Lord, we suffer—and trials are a wake-up call.

When things went from bad to worse, Jonah realized that his change of circumstances did not cure his pain; it only compounded his problems. He delayed his obedience, and others were hurt in the wake of his wandering away from God. We put our faith at risk when we are not faithful. We let down those closest to us and rupture our relationships. Unless we wake up to the reality that *we* are the problem, problems will persist. Owning our wrongs helps us make things right. Trials can bring us back to trusting the Lord and motivate us to earn back the trust of others.

"Love the Lord, all his faithful people! The Lord preserves those who are true to him, but the proud he pays back in full."

PSALM 31:23

Heavenly Father, thank You for choosing me. Grow me more into the likeness of Your Son. Prune out of my heart distorted loves, and replace them with sweet affection for You. Renew my mind with the truth of Your love, so in turn I can love others like You love me.

63

Even in the Broken Parts

The Spirit of the Sovereign Lord is on me, because the Lord has anointed me to proclaim good news to the poor. He has sent me to bind up the brokenhearted, to proclaim freedom for the captives and release from darkness for the prisoners.

ISAIAH 61:1

For those who have lost a loved one, we know what it's like to walk through the valley of the shadow of death. Likely we can all agree it is the darkest valley we've ever been in. Yet Psalm 23:4 says, "Even though I walk through the darkest valley, I will fear no evil, for you are with me; your rod and your staff, they comfort me." The words refer to protection and comfort. Even when we find ourselves in the darkest valley, God still walks alongside us, carrying us through the darkness … even in the broken parts of our story.

Death and grief can grab us like nothing else in life does. They change the innermost parts of our being and make us question everything around us—everything we thought to be true.

Trusting God, especially during the most challenging times, is not only the hardest thing to do but the most essential. As we continue to walk what may feel like a desert road, if we give the journey to God, we will become stronger. We can place the broken parts of our hearts into the hands of the One who made us and trust that He will make all things new. Somehow He takes all that has been broken and shifts it into something beautiful and good. Even in the broken parts, He is in our story.

"You are my hiding place; you will protect
me from trouble and surround
me with songs of deliverance.
I will instruct you and teach you in the
way you should go; I will counsel
you with my loving eye on you."

PSALM 32:7-8

Heavenly Father, You alone can heal
every part of my brokenness. Especially
during the broken parts of my story,
I look to You to make me whole again.

64

TRIALS RESULTING FROM ANOTHER'S CHOICES

So, when Joseph arrived, his brothers ripped off the beautiful robe he was wearing. Then they grabbed him and threw him into the cistern.

GENESIS 37:23-24, NLT

The Lord was with Joseph is a phrase used each time Joseph encountered a new trial that was initiated by someone else's decision. The jealousy of his brothers boiled over into anger and the violent act of tossing Joseph into a pit to die. Then they decided to make money instead and sold him as a slave to a traveling band of traders. But *the Lord was with Joseph.* The hardworking, handsome young man was sold to Potiphar to manage his household. Joseph worked hard, with spectacular success. Driven by lust, Potiphar's wife tried to seduce Joseph but failed, so she falsely accused him of rape. Unjustly, he went to prison, but *the Lord was with Joseph.*

Your trial may be a disease you did not see coming. Storms sometimes blow through, and trees uproot and fall, causing great damage to a home. Another person's foolish decisions may have you financially strapped or emotionally trapped. A fallen world can be cruel and severe in its disruption of lives and property. But *the Lord is still with you.* Fortunately, one day Jesus will restore to His followers a new earth, flourishing and without sin. Allow the trials that come from the choices of others to make your faith stronger as you wait for that day.

"Consider it pure joy, my brothers and sisters, whenever you face trials of many kinds, because you know that the testing of your faith produces perseverance."

JAMES 1:2-3

Heavenly Father, give me the grace to forgive others who have brought a season of suffering into my life. Search my heart and show me who I need to forgive, even if they do not deserve my forgiveness. Deliver me from a resentful heart and replace it with a grateful heart.

65

Grief and Gratitude

This is the day the Lord has made.
We will rejoice and be glad in it.

PSALM 118:24, NLT

Joining grief and gratitude together seems like an oxymoron, doesn't it? Although it may be unimaginable, grief and gratitude can begin to coexist together. When we were learning to swim, we didn't just jump in the deep end of the pool and start swimming twenty laps. No, as we reached the surface, we were likely sputtering and thrashing around. Grief can be similar. We will not wake up the day after the funeral and be ready to step into gratitude. This is a process over time that is different for everyone. We can begin by honoring and celebrating the positive memories of our loved one's life rather than focusing on the negative emotions of their loss—when we are ready.

This doesn't mean we won't have moments of sadness or that we won't miss the person we lost. But practicing gratitude can help us deal with our emotions and improve our mental health. Sorrow is not a sin, and gratitude does not cancel out grief. Living in grief and gratitude is not about being grateful when someone we love dies. The concept is more deeply rooted in being grateful for our time with our loved ones while being thankful for the memories that remain with us after their death. When we begin to practice living in gratitude, it allows us to begin healing from our pain and suffering and is a transformative way of dealing with loss.

"And let the peace of Christ rule in your hearts, since as members of one body you were called to peace. And be thankful."

COLOSSIANS 3:15

Father, thank You for helping me learn how to find gratitude in my grief. It's a challenging task, but I trust You to be the driver of this difficult road.

66

Trials as a Test of Integrity

Then the Lord asked Satan, "Have you noticed my servant Job? He is the finest man in all the earth. He is blameless— a man of complete integrity."

JOB 1:8, NLT

Job was a man of integrity who feared God and avoided evil. He was blameless. Remarkably, he did not curse God or blame the devil, despite his dire circumstances. His children died, his business went bust, his fortune evaporated, and his wife and closest friends lost faith in him. But Job endured these hellish conditions, never losing hope in God to bring healing and restoration. The blessing of still trusting in the Lord during his deep trial meant that his intimacy with God grew deeper. Job learned things about God's love and power that he may have missed in less severe days. He passed the test of integrity by patiently processing in prayer and leaning into the Lord.

You may be experiencing a test of your integrity. Will you continue to do the right thing when you have been treated wrongly? Is your faith contingent on everything going well, or on the

an outward sign that He lived and died for us. This can give us a different perspective on our own scars. With the loss, we will carry scars, but one day these wounds will be gone forever. We can see these as a sign that we lived and survived through good and bad times. One day the scars we carry will no longer be.

"Yes, we are of good courage, and we would rather be away from the body and at home with the Lord."

2 CORINTHIANS 5:8, ESV

Father God, my hope remains in You as I walk through this life with scars. I look forward to the day You return with joy, anticipating being reunited with my loved ones. On that day You will remove every scar from my heart.

68

Holy Spirit Strength

And Christ lives within you, so even though your body will die because of sin, the Spirit gives you life because you have been made right with God.

ROMANS 8:10, NLT

The apostle Paul, by engaging with eternal resources, experienced boundless energy. Though emotionally torn between *knowing the right thing to do* but *still doing the wrong thing*, he remained steadfast in leaning into the love of God to keep him secure in the Spirit's strength. Physically beaten and left for dead outside a city, he reached deep down into his soul, maybe reflecting on his Lord's gruesome death on the cross—and stood up and made his way back into the city to share the good news of Christ's resurrection from the dead. The Holy Spirit gives life.

As the winds of adversity threaten your security, keep the flag of your faith raised high, and watch with the eyes of your soul which direction the Holy Spirit is blowing. Challenges in life can accelerate your understanding of God's will for your life, so follow confidently, knowing the Lord knows best. It may be only when you look into the rearview mirror of time that you are able to see what the Spirit was preparing for you. The Father is your fortress, Jesus is your friend, and the Spirit is your strength and guide. Keep moving forward by faith, submitted to and strengthened by the Holy Spirit.

"You are my strength; I wait for you to rescue me, for you, O God, are my fortress. In his unfailing love, my God will stand with me."

PSALM 59:9-10, NLT

Heavenly Father, strengthen and lead me by Your Spirit; through Christ's love, help me face my challenges by following the Spirit's lead and making hard decisions when necessary. Use my challenges in life to accelerate Your will for my life so I confidently know Your ways.

69

Grief, Grit, and Grace

But he said to me, "My grace is sufficient for you, for my power is made perfect in weakness." Therefore I will boast all the more gladly about my weaknesses, so that Christ's power may rest on me.

2 CORINTHIANS 12:9

Grief, grit, and grace are three different words but, in many ways, complementary to one another. While grieving my daughter's death, someone once told me I had a lot of grit. I knew what defined grief—*sorrow, misery, anguish, and pain*—all facets of grief I keenly possessed. But grit? It was an interesting term. After looking up the definition, *grit* means having courage, resolve, and character strength. Now, I wouldn't consider myself a naturally courageous person, but when child loss becomes woven into the fabric of the tapestry of your life, do you really have a choice to be anything other than courageous?

When someone you love dies, it would be easy to fold like a deck of cards and never get up again. But we can pick ourselves up and begin walking forward, no matter the circumstances. If we look at this from a different angle, because of what we've lived through, we can share the lessons we've learned along the way and positively uplift and encourage others who find themselves grieving. As a person of faith, I yearn to continually have the character quality of grace, which means *to honor, enhance, and extend courtesy*. I need to give grace not just to myself, but also to others. Giving grace has been one of those lessons grief has taught me. I have learned to view people and their circumstances differently. The things I once thought were so important are not so much anymore. The more important things aren't things at all, but people. I treasure the time and relationships with those God has placed in my life.

"But to each one of us grace has been given as Christ apportioned it."

EPHESIANS 4:7

Lord, thank You for the gifts of grace and grit. Thank You for teaching me to extend grace toward others and make beauty from the ashes.

70

From Grumbling to Gratitude

Moses and Aaron told the People of Israel, "This evening you will know that it is God who brought you out of Egypt; and in the morning you will see the Glory of God. Yes, he's listened to your complaints against him. You haven't been complaining against us, you know, but against God."

EXODUS 16:6-7, MSG

Are you tempted to not trust the Lord because of a trial or test you face? If so, remind yourself of His track record of faithfulness. Once you were blind to the grace and love of Jesus, but now you can see how He has led you in love to experience total forgiveness and acceptance in your beloved Savior and Lord. When you encountered Christ, you came face-to-face with the One who has your back, especially during a spiritual dry time. Just like your merciful Father wooed you to Himself before you tasted His satisfying salvation, so He still woos you back to His table of grace. Fear requires you to check boxes of performance; grace reminds you that all boxes were checked on the cross. We can now rest and be ever grateful to God for the rich relationships that He has kindly brought into our lives. Glad gratitude replaces sad grumbling.

Of course, there are times to bring our complaints to God. Jesus even lamented, "Why have you forsaken me?" (Matthew 27:46). Our life in Christ does not consist of chronic complaining, but on occasion, we do bring our grumblings to God, and He graciously meets us with gentle doses of His love to revive our hearts and remind us of His generous blessings. Trials and tests are preparation for the promised land of abundant living. Convert grumbling into gratitude!

"Friends, don't complain about each other. A far greater complaint could be lodged against you, you know. The Judge is standing just around the corner."

JAMES 5:9, MSG

Heavenly Father, replace my grumbling heart with a grateful heart through Christ's love. Help me see that trials and tests are preparation for the promised land of abundant living and thanksgiving. I am truly thankful for Your tremendous blessings that fill my life.

71

The Many Faces of Grief

My flesh and my heart may fail,
but God is the strength of
my heart and my portion forever.

PSALM 73:26

Grief is defined as deep and poignant distress. This is true, but as we walk this journey, there are many different faces of grief. During the early days, there is often a sadness and hollowness deep within. Darkness, disbelief, and distress can consume our every thought. After a while, grief can begin to take on another face—the face of loneliness. The missing and longing for what was and what could have been go hand in hand like soul sisters. These are all normal responses to grief, yet there does come a time when the face begins to change. The darkness will not always be so dark, and the pain will not always be so sharp.

Only One can bring the balm we need to heal our broken hearts; His name is Jesus. His promise to us in Psalm 23:3-6 in *The Message* sums it up so well: "True to your word, you let me catch my breath and send me in the right direction. Even when the way goes through Death Valley, I'm not afraid when you walk by my side … You revive my drooping head; my cup brims with blessing. Your beauty and love chase after me every day of my life." Wow! Such hope for a weary soul! Gratefully we will begin to see the other faces of grief: Compassion. Understanding. Empathy. Each one brings a bit more hope during our loss.

"So also you have sorrow now, but I will see you again, and your hearts will rejoice, and no one will take your joy from you."

JOHN 16:22, ESV

Father, Your blessings to us are many, but none are so great as Your presence when we are walking through Death Valley. On the valley floor, we feel Your strength as You lift up Your children, carrying us through the darkest days. Thank You for being our loving Father.

72

Compassion in Grief

For no one is abandoned by the Lord forever. Though he brings grief, he also shows compassion because of the greatness of his unfailing love.

LAMENTATIONS 3:31-32, NLT

Jeremiah was familiar with grief—multi-faceted grief. The grief of personal shame. The grief of rejection. The grief of relational loss. The grief of financial loss. The grief of a nation on its knees, suffering from the destruction of its once impenetrable walls of protection. Exiled and estranged from the life they had once taken for granted, the people of God learned to live for God in a land not their own. A dislocation from familiar settings facilitated a fierce faith. Love grew out of the ashes of adversity. The walls of Jerusalem fell, but those who looked up saw hope, healing, and heaven. The Lord shows compassion in the depths of our grief.

Your life may be cut down to the stump, but don't allow despair to be a stump grinder. Look for the green sprout of God's compassion to nurture your heart with hope. Enjoy a richer intimacy with your Savior, Jesus. Let the roots of your righteous life go deeper into the rich soil of the Lord's love.

Water your soul with weepy eyes and a tender heart. Your grief is wrapped in the compassion of Christ, as a resurrected life follows death—the Spirit gives you strength for life's journey!

"For I am about to do something new. See, I have already begun! Do you not see it?"

ISAIAH 43:19, NLT

Dear precious Jesus, I am afraid; I am sad; help me to process my grief through Your love, mercy, and comfort. Your grace is greater than my pain. I love You and place all my hope in You right now. Mourning is the medicine I am drinking in, for my laments to draw me closer to Your loving compassion.

73

A Broken Heart Still Beats

Peace I leave with you; my peace I give you. I do not give to you as the world gives. Do not your hearts be troubled and do not be afraid.

JOHN 14:27

When I was told that my daughter died, it took my heart a moment to catch up with the words my ears heard. How does the body manage to keep living when the worst thing that could happen to you occurs? The first thing I felt was shock, followed by numbness. I'm convinced this is the body's way of protecting itself. As the hours passed, I began to absorb the enormity of the situation. I was sure my heart wouldn't survive. But I discovered that somehow, a broken heart still beats. The sun rises in the morning every day, and the moon appears in the night sky when the day is over.

Some people think we are strong because we managed to survive the loss of our loved one. But really, what choice did we have? Others ask, how do you do it? I attribute every step taken along this journey to my faith in God. That doesn't mean it's been easy, and it's not always pretty. Healing a broken heart is messy and complicated work. But when our hearts are devastated, if we can put our life in our heavenly Father's hands, we will not just go through the motions of life; He will help us to actually live again. He is the healer of all broken things (Isaiah 41:10). Placing our brokenness into the hands of the One who made us is our only hope. There is no specific time frame for grief. Just don't give up. Reach out to the One who longs to hold on to you, and He will carry your broken heart that still beats in His gentle, loving hands.

"Don't be afraid, for I am with you.
Don't be discouraged, for I am your God.
I will strengthen you and help you.
I will hold you up with my victorious right hand."

ISAIAH 41:10, NLT

Father, thank You for being the healer of all broken things. I wholeheartedly trust in You, especially during my life's messy, challenging moments.

74

When Bad Things Happen, Stay Faithful to God

We count as blessed those who have persevered. You have heard of Job's perseverance and have seen what the Lord finally brought about. The Lord is full of compassion and mercy.

JAMES 5:11

Job never blamed God for his bad—some would even say horrific—circumstances. His hope was still in heaven, even if the Lord took him to heaven. Faithfulness to Christ is not based on your circumstances or even on your perception of injustice. Faithfulness happens when you choose to see the bigger picture of your Fathers heart's desire for what is best for you. No loss is wasted with the Lord's love. Stay faithful in the face of adversity and trust that He is at work. The Lord's compassion and mercy are near to the brokenhearted to administer His healing love.

Pain is your opportunity to look up for help and cry out to your Creator for His comfort and love. God's power to create the world is your reminder of His power to shepherd you through the threats of disease or fear of the unknown. When someone asks how you are, instead of a glib "fine," take inventory of your hurting heart and confess that you have Feelings on the Inside that Need Expressing (F.I.N.E.). Your sympathizing Savior understands. Hallelujah, you can worship Him, caught up in His holy love.

"For he guards the course of the just and protects the way of his faithful ones."

PROVERBS 2:8

Father of all comfort, I praise You that because of Your great love, I am not consumed, and Your compassions never fail. They are new every morning, and great is Your faithfulness. Thank You for being faithful to me, even when I am unfaithful to You. Keep my heart steadfast, trusting in Your love.

75

Accepting the Life We Didn't Choose

May the God who gives endurance and encouragement give you the same attitude of mind toward each other that Christ Jesus had, so that with one mind and one voice you may glorify the God and Father of our Lord Jesus Christ. Accept one another, then, just as Christ accepted you, in order to bring praise to God.

ROMANS 15:5-7

When the world around you falls apart and you're completely blindsided by life, you may wonder where God is. Many people cry out to Him when life goes awry, while others wonder if God exists. We think, *if He were here, how could He let* this *happen?* When we find ourselves in sorrow and loss, these questions often come to mind. If we had our choice, our loved ones would still be here. Living. Breathing. Experiencing life with us. Yet time stops for no one, and as hard as loss is, there will come a day when we must accept the life we didn't choose.

When death comes knocking on our door, we must figure out where we go from here. Giving up is not an option. Even through the hardest of times, our faith can sustain us. It comes down to trust, faith, and hope. Trust that God is who He says He is. Have faith that His Word is true. And hold on to the hope we have in Christ. We may not understand the why of this chapter in our story, but accepting the life we didn't choose can open the door, allowing God to use this part of our story in ways we never imagined. Our thoughts are not God's thoughts, and His ways are higher than ours (Isaiah 55:8-9). So let us continue to rely on and trust in Him as we also continue to accept this part of our life that we would not have chosen for ourselves.

"Let me see your kindness to me in the morning, for I am trusting you. Show me where to walk, for my prayer is sincere."

PSALM 143:8, TLB

Jesus, even when I don't understand Your ways, I am committed to trusting You with my life. Lead me through the darkness into Your everlasting light.

76

When Bad Things Happen, Worship God

At this, Job got up and tore his robe and shaved his head. Then he fell to the ground to worship.

JOB 1:20

Are you struggling to understand? Are you stuck in a state of anger? Have you lost something or someone very precious? It may be the loss of your child's health or even the death of a child. A spouse may have gone to heaven or left you for someone else. Your children may be angry because they do not understand why you are divorcing. They want their parents to work it out so they can have a mom and dad. Is your heart hemorrhaging with hurt and animosity?

Worship the Lord in your pain and loss. It is healing to focus on the greatness, holiness, and wonder of God. Praise Him with your voice and praise Him with your heart and mind. You may need to let a caring friend cradle you in their arms and sing softly in your ear, "Great Is Thy Faithfulness" and "Jesus Loves Me." This song sums it up well: "Turn your eyes upon Jesus; look full into his wonderful face. And the things of earth will grow strangely dim in the light of His glory and grace." Worship God in the middle of your pain and worry; by faith, receive the wonders of His grace!

"Come, let us bow down in worship,
let us kneel before the Lord our Maker."

PSALM 95:6

Heavenly Father, I praise and worship You in the glory of Your presence and peace. Lead me to be creative to engage in the regular personal and corporate worship of Your wonder and glory. May my praise to You be a pillow of rest to my head and peace to my heart.

77

Grief Impacts More than the Heart

Praise be to the God and Father of our Lord Jesus Christ, the Father of compassion and the God of all comfort, who comforts us in all our troubles, so that we can comfort those in any trouble with the comfort we ourselves receive from God.

2 CORINTHIANS 1:3-4

When we think of grief's impact on us, our emotions come to mind first—sadness, loneliness, the desperate missing, and mourning of our loved ones. But really, it's so much bigger than that. Grief impacts so much more than our hearts. Do you feel tired all the time? Does your energy seem to have vanished? Does your mind wander, and you can't remain focused? Do you walk into a room and wonder why you even went there? If this sounds familiar and these things are happening to you, be encouraged. There is nothing wrong with you. My friends, this is grief!

So what can you do? First and foremost, be kind and gentle with yourself, giving yourself grace. Consider not overscheduling yourself, and learn to say, "No, thank you. I'd love to, but I can't." Try your best to get a good night's sleep or incorporate a short nap into your day if your schedule allows. Developing alternative habits to assist with the brain fog accompanying grief helps too. Write things down immediately, and don't rely on your memory, as this can cause frustration when your thoughts vanish into thin air like the wind. We are human and shouldn't be so hard on ourselves. The grief journey is chock full of twists and turns. Try to develop a habit of giving yourself some quiet time—perhaps begin each morning with just you and Jesus. Placing our hope, faith, and trust in Him makes a difference in our walk. He can do all that we cannot do for ourselves. He is able!

"A happy heart makes the face cheerful,
but heartache crushes the spirit."

PROVERBS 15:13

Father, thank You for wanting every part of my being to be healed and happy. There isn't one part of me that You do not care for. Thank You for increasing my joy and peace along this rocky road.

78

He Gives and He Takes

Naked I came from my mother's womb,
and naked I will depart. The Lord
gave and the Lord has taken away;
may the name of the Lord be praised.

JOB 1:21

It is easy to praise God when He gives you good things, but it is hard to praise Him when He takes away good things. Yet, it is the power of praise to the Lord that empowers your faith to endure. Praise to Jesus prompts you to persevere in belief and obedience. He realigns your heart and mind to embrace heaven's expectations instead of bowing to earth's demands. When God gives, it's a blessing; when He takes, it's a blessing. He knows your needs and will not leave you alone.

You can be content and grateful for the lot in life God has given you. Perhaps He has you in your current career for the growth of your character and competence. Sometimes He rains down grace, and other times the sun of adversity beats down in a sweat of suffering. The Lord gives and takes in His timing and for His glory. Hold loosely His blessings and burdens and be ready to receive His great grace and love. Everything in the heavens and earth is His—to use at His discretion.

"What is your life? You are a mist that appears for a little while and then vanishes. Instead, you ought to say, 'If it is the Lord's will, we will live and do this or that.'"

JAMES 4:14-15

Heavenly Father, I trust You in all seasons—when You give and when You take. Show me what I need to let go of that You may be taking away. Realign my heart and mind to heaven's expectations instead of bowing to earth's demands. For me, to live is Christ—to die is gain.

79

How Long Will the Grief Last?

He will give a crown of beauty for ashes,
a joyous blessing instead of mourning,
festive praise instead of despair.

ISAIAH 61:3, NLT

One day, at the end of a speaking engagement, a woman came rushing up to me and burst out, "Are you over it yet? How long will this grief last?" Although it took me by surprise momentarily, the question came from a pure and sincere place. It took only a moment to let her know I was not entirely over my grief, and I didn't think I ever would be. If that sounds hopeless to you, please stay with me, because this is not the end of the story. Just as the ocean's waves vary, grief changes, but it never totally disappears from one's life.

Later I found out the woman had been pressured by others to be over her loss. This is a good reminder that there is no time line for grief, and we each walk this journey in our own way. Some days it is quiet, and others, it bubbles up for no apparent reason. But it's always there, simmering just below the surface like a geyser waiting to erupt. Try to focus on the good times and the love you shared. Your grief will eventually become a part of you, like the color of your eyes or hair. We can be grateful for the lighter, softer days that have evolved from the broken, jagged pieces and look forward to a day when there will be no more sadness and tears. As time progresses, God can take our broken pieces and transform them into something new. He uses our brokenness to create something good and beautiful, all in His time.

"In their hearts humans plan their course,
but the Lord establishes their steps."

PROVERBS 16:9

Lord, I'm so grateful that Your timing
is perfect. Even when the way is hard
and I long for the sadness of my grief
to be gone, I know You are with me
as I take each breath, waiting for You
to turn these ashes into beauty.

80

Die in the Lord

We, too, writhe in agony, but nothing comes of our suffering. We have not given salvation to the earth, nor brought life into the world. But those who die in the Lord will live; their bodies will rise again!

ISAIAH 26:18-19, NLT

The prophet Isaiah captures the sobering imagery of suffering, the agony of death, the feelings of frustration for not being able to save the earth or human life from its cruel conditions. God's wisdom brings the spiritual giant of his day back to God—the Author of life and death. God's salvation for the dying offers eternal life to those who die in the Lord. Your Creator lovingly observes the groans of His creation and will one day reign over a new heaven and a new earth.

Are you ready to meet the Lord? Have you made peace with God? Those who have peace with God experience the peace of God. Peace is evidence that you will die in the Lord. When all you have is Christ alone, you can better learn to trust Christ alone. Use a crisis to move beyond your doubt and embrace an authentic faith tried by fire, and you will be found faithful.

You are buried with Him in baptism and raised to walk in the newness of life—ready to die in the Lord.

"Or have you forgotten that when we were joined with Christ Jesus in baptism, we joined him in his death? For we died and were buried with Christ by baptism."

ROMANS 6:3-4, NLT

Dear Lord, I praise You for the assurance of being with me in this life and in my ultimate death. Show me the authenticity of my faith as I die to my self-reliance and place my faith totally in You. Help me grow old with grace so the shadow of my life influence points others to You.

81

Growing Through Grief

I am the vine, you are the branches. He who abides in Me, and I in him, bears much fruit; or without Me you can do nothing.

JOHN 15:5, NKJV

Just like a summer rainstorm can come out of nowhere on a beautiful sunny day, there are days when the waves of grief can suddenly threaten to consume you. During the first year, it's normal to encounter a sea of emotions that hits without warning. It ebbs and flows, just like the waves of the ocean. As we experience all the firsts without our loved one, we also reflect on all the lasts, remembering what was … the last hug, the last birthday, the last anniversary, and particularly, the last words. As you reflect, take a moment to look at how far you've come since that first day when your world changed. Eventually, you will realize the frequency of those tsunami-force waves is occurring less frequently and with less intensity. Now when they crash over you, they might make you stumble, but you don't feel like you're drowning.

We grow through our grief. We do this by grasping hold of our faith, like a person who can't swim clings to a life preserver when they've been thrown into the middle of the ocean. God is our shield and strength. We continue to run to Him on those days when we feel like we're going under. Like a teenager who has growing pains through adolescence, we have growing pains through our grief journey. One day you will look up and see that you're stronger than you ever thought possible, all because you held on to Jesus through the storm.

"So we say with confidence, 'The Lord is my helper; I will not be afraid. What can mere mortals do to me?'"

HEBREWS 13:6

Sweet Jesus, I'm ever so comforted by knowing You are my shield and the One who walks with me as I experience the growing pains of grief. I'm confident You walk alongside and lift me when the waves threaten to take me under. Thank You for being my protector in the storm.

82

Sorrow and Your Savior

He will swallow up death forever. The Sovereign Lord will wipe away the tears from all faces; he will remove his people's disgrace from all the earth. The Lord has spoken.

ISAIAH 25:8

Sorrow is the fruit of sin in a fallen world; the darkness is at liberty to inflict pain. No one is immune from sorrow. Sorrow is created by sin, death, divorce, selfishness, poverty, rejection, loss, and fear. Sorrow is all around, and it circles its prey like vultures around a carcass, ready to pick away at the meat of your soul. Sorrow does not discriminate among races, gender, social class, or stage of life. It causes a weepy heart and a weary mind over a lifetime. Your sorrow may be overwhelming to the point of anguish and despair. The hurt is about to drive you crazy. You feel as if you can't handle it. Things have gone from bad to worse; you have nowhere to turn.

Prayer is the medication of God's grace. Administer larger doses in the beginning to stop the spread of sorrow's infection. He wants you to experience abundant life in Christ. He wipes away your tears in heaven and on earth. Let God remove your points of pain one by one as if they were trees downed by a storm's horrific winds. Sorrow is temporary with God; His joy is permanent. Let Jesus remove your sorrow, for He is the Savior of your sorrows.

"He was despised and rejected by mankind, a man of suffering, and familiar with pain."

ISAIAH 53:3

Jesus, thank You that You are the Man of Sorrows who understands and heals. Spread Your mercy and grace over my wounded heart and battered body. I need Your comfort and the comfort of Your children who are familiar with my pain. My tears are a tribute to Your love.

83

The Gratitude Journal

Give thanks to the Lord, for he is good.
His love endures forever.

PSALM 136:1

A friend gifted me a gratitude journal during the early days of grief. My friend had such good and kind intentions, but I wasn't in a place where I could appreciate it. My heart wasn't ready to give gratitude and thanks when I felt so sad. One day a couple of years later, I was searching for something, and what did I find in the back of my drawer? The gratitude journal. I sat down and took a few minutes to read through it. Seeing that journal reminded me of how God had been carrying me through my grief. He had slowly and tenderly taken me from those early days when life was so very dark and each day was filled with such heart-wrenching emotions, to a place where I could feel His warmth and could see the cracks of light through the brokenness.

Discovering the journal reminded me how much I genuinely have to be grateful for. It's hard to see gratitude when your heart is shattered by loss. When we lose someone we love, getting our feet back under us takes a long time. If you're still walking through your grief journey where the weight of it all is heavy, please let this encourage you. Eventually, life can be good again. Grief will always be a part of us, but if we allow it, our faith can heal our deepest hurts.

"Give thanks in all circumstances; for this is God's will for you in Christ Jesus."

1 THESSALONIANS 5:18

Jesus, if I had written in that gratitude journal, I would have told You how grateful I am for Your love and how my faith in You is the only thing that has sustained me. I'm thankful for how You can bring comfort and peace to a broken heart and spirit. Thank You for putting my broken pieces back together again.

84

Healing Hurt

Therefore confess your sins to each other and pray for each other so that you may be healed. The prayer of a righteous person is powerful and effective.

JAMES 5:16

How do we handle deep hurts that have compounded in crazy cycles over many years? Where do we go when the hurt is so unbearable that we stay scared, implode in anger, and grow a root of bitterness? Fortunately, there is a very real hope for healing found in our loving heavenly Father and His caring children. Healing doesn't happen by accident, but begins with an intentional acknowledgment of the need for wholeness by God's grace.

Through faith in Jesus Christ as your Lord and Savior, you are a precious child of God. He died for you. You are loved by the Lord and by His loving children. Confess your desperate need for His love and forgiveness. Linger long in the accepting arms of Jesus and let Him love you. You are not alone. He was rejected so you could be accepted. He served so you can serve and be served. He died so you can live. His grace heals. Listen to the gracious words of others who love the Lord. What they say is sincere and true. Reject the lies of the devil and his followers, and embrace the healing truth of trusted friends and counselors. Emotions can betray, but truth will keep you from straying.

"Gracious words are a honeycomb, sweet to the soul and healing to the bones."

PROVERBS 16:24

Heavenly Father, bring healing to my wounded heart and teach me to forgive. Show me the hurts in my heart that I need to say out loud and receive Your love and healing for. I praise You that Your grace heals and Your truth reveals how my gracious words can be healing to others.

85

Invite Grief and Gratitude to the Table

Be strong and courageous. Do not be afraid or terrified because of them, for the Lord your God goes with you; he will never leave you nor forsake you.

DEUTERONOMY 31:6

How often do we don our masks, paste on a fake smile, and tell everyone we are doing fine, while inside we may be feeling anything but? Maybe you feel pressured to behave in a certain way to meet others' expectations of how you should be at this point in your grief journey. You smile on the outside, when inside, your heart is broken. Instead of pretending, let's invite grief and gratitude to the table. Yes, it will take courage to take this step, but just like Peter stepped out of the boat toward Jesus during the storm, you can do it! We do not have to act a certain way or be someone we aren't just to appease others or make those around us feel more comfortable.

One of the greatest lessons we can learn is that grief and gratitude can coexist. You can have both joy and sorrow in your heart. So instead of acting as if everything is perfect, be vulnerable and be your most authentic self. If you want to share about your loved one, do so with boldness and all the love you have in your heart for them. Mentioning their name and telling stories involving our loved ones helps keep them alive. It doesn't bring sadness when we talk about them, but rather brings us joy to know they have not been forgotten. We may shed a tear one moment and have a burst of laughter the next. That's OK. This is a step along the journey toward healing.

"Be strong and take heart,
all you who hope in the Lord."

PSALM 31:24

Lord, help me to look inside and see the lion's heart You have given me. Thank You for giving me courage like David and helping me walk in Your might and power, because it is through You that I can do everything.

86

Relational Repair

"Lord," he said, "my servant lies at home paralyzed, suffering terribly." Jesus said to him, "Shall I come and heal him?"

MATTHEW 8:6-7

Jesus illustrates grace in His response to the request of a man most despised by the Jewish people. This Roman soldier, who had inflicted pain and suffering on Christ's contemporaries, asked Jesus for the healing of one of his prized slaves. This powerful centurion unapologetically asked a favor from one who represented a people persecuted by this leader and his government. Jesus chose healing over hate. He restored the relationship. The Lord served a man who easily could have been viewed as an enemy, and chose to grow his faith.

Relationships are like cars—from time to time, they break down. If we ignore the regular maintenance of relational repair, it will be to our peril. Marriage, parenting, work, family, and friends all require ongoing evaluation and consistent investment of time and energy. It is especially necessary for us to prayerfully look for ways to serve those whom we have hurt or who have hurt us. Relational repair doesn't mean a perfect relationship, but one that applies love to the wound. It requires ongoing conversation to restore trust and intimacy. God's grace leads to confession and repentance, which positions us for relational healing with our heavenly Father and with others. He reciprocates with love, forgiveness, and reconciliation with Him that we can extend to others.

"Be kind and compassionate to one another, forgiving each other, just as in Christ God forgave you."

EPHESIANS 4:32

Heavenly Father, give me the humble initiative to serve those who have hurt me or whom I have hurt. Lead me to those I need to forgive or who need to forgive me for insensitive remarks or an uncaring attitude. In Your love, help us to have ongoing conversations to restore trust and intimacy.

87

The Never-Ending Journey of Grief and Healing

I will not leave you comfortless:
I will come to you.

JOHN 14:18, KJV

When loss touches your life, no matter how many days, months, or years go by, there will always be a piece of your heart that remains on the never-ending grief journey. But don't be discouraged! Even knowing this, be comforted by knowing that the Healer of your heart walks with you in the grief. He has many names and answers to them all when you call Him. His name is Jesus, Father, Comforter, Friend, Brother, Holy One, and God. Through the wonder of it all, we walk this journey side-by-side, whether in the valley or on the mountaintop. He is never-ending in the most beautiful sense. He is faithful, forever, limitless, unending, and always on the journey with you.

God, in all His magnificence, covers, comforts, and carries us when we think we won't make it another day. He is the Healer of our hearts. Just like any other deep wound, healing our hearts will take time, along with a lot of grief work. While time may not heal all wounds, time lessens the overwhelming, sharp, bitter feelings early grief brings. If you're hurting today and missing your loved one, I encourage you to hold on, don't give up, and keep running to the Father.

"God is not human, that he should lie, not a human being, that he should change his mind. Does he speak and then not act? Does he promise and not fulfill?"

NUMBERS 23:19

As the song goes, "Oh Lord, our Lord, how majestic is Your name in all the earth!" How blessed are we that we can call out Your name, and You hear us and come running. Even when sadness seems to be on every side, I place my trust in You. When You say that weeping may endure for a night, but joy comes in the morning, I believe it because You are the Word, and You are truth.

88

Elevated Thinking

"For my thoughts are not your thoughts, neither are your ways my ways," declares the Lord.

ISAIAH 55:8

God's will does not always make sense. It may not make sense because we factor in our own understanding. If left to our own understanding, we would be miserable. There is a greater pool of knowledge reserved for us in Christ; do not underestimate its value and availability. It is valuable because of the divine direction that can save us from running down paths that waste our time and the time of others. God's way may not make sense to us now, but it will later. His thoughts and ways are easily accessible by faith. Elevated thinking can grow into eternal thinking.

The mind of Christ gives you an advantage. You do not have to think inaccurate thoughts. You may currently believe something that is untrue. You may believe God does not love you and will not forgive you. This is not true. He loves you right where you are, and He desires His very best for you. God's best is best. Why settle for anything less? Think God-sized thoughts and expect God-sized results. Make His ways your ways; incorporate His thinking into your thinking. It may seem peculiar at first. Others may label you as strange, but you know better. Eternal thinking is elevated thinking, and when your thinking is right, you can't go wrong.

"'Who can know the Lord's thoughts?
Who knows enough to teach him?'
But we understand these things,
for we have the mind of Christ."

1 CORINTHIANS 2:16, NLT

Heavenly Father, I seek Your wisdom from above so I can make wise decisions here below. Lead me to those I can ask for wise counsel, so I am more objective and not just led by my feelings. When Your will doesn't make sense to me, reassure me by Your Spirit's comfort, peace, and guidance.

89

Practicing the 3 C's of Grief: Choose, Connect, Communicate

You did not choose Me, but I chose you and appointed you that you should go and bear fruit, and that your fruit should remain, that whatever you ask the Father in My name He may give you.

John 15:16, NKJV

The grief journey isn't a sprint; it's a marathon. We will not get through our grief in 1 minute, 20 seconds. No, it takes time and work. We can begin practicing the 3 C's of grief for hurting people: Choose, Connect, and Communicate. First, we get to choose what is best for us. When we have lost a loved one, we may feel like we've lost control over our lives and have no choice. But even when our hearts are heavy and burdened, we still possess the dignity of choice. Grief brain is a real thing, and if you find that your brain is muddied and cloudy and you really can't think clearly, engage the help of a close friend or family member. You still have the final say and can choose what is best for you as you navigate this journey.

Grief in and of itself can be very isolating and exacerbate feelings of loneliness. Even if you are a total introvert and usually enjoy your own company, you need to connect with people during this challenging time because it's crucial to our mind and well-being. Although no one can fix your grief, just having another person present, without saying a word, can help immeasurably. We are not meant to do this life alone. Jesus took time to step away from the crowds, but He always came back. He knew He couldn't accomplish all God had for Him alone. Lastly, communicate and share openly and honestly about your needs and what works best for you right now. It will help your friends and family know how best to come alongside you.

"Wait for the Lord; be strong and take heart and wait for the Lord."

PSALM 27:14

Lord, You know how complicated grief is. We cannot do this alone. Please help us to navigate the course, since this road doesn't have GPS guidance. Heavenly Father, our hope is solely in You.

90

Struggling to Die

Some time later the woman's son became sick. He grew worse and worse, and finally he died.

1 KINGS 17:17, NLT

Elijah, the famous Old Testament prophet, loved a widow and her sick son well. Childhood disease seems so unfair, even cruel, yet this man of God provided hope and physical provision as the young man's health gradually deteriorated. The mom's faith in God was severely tested as each day she watched her precious boy waste away. The outer shell of his life tarnished more and more, while the inner soul glistened more and more in the light of the Lord's love. The mom must have prayed, "Dear merciful God, take my son or heal him so he doesn't have to suffer." He finally died, but hope was very much alive. God, through the prophet, breathed life into the son.

Maybe a loved one is terminal, but you don't know the time they have left—maybe months, maybe years. Make the most of the time you have and avoid obsessing in fear of what the future might hold. Be grateful to God for the opportunity to hold him one more day before the day he goes away. Invite the community of Christ's followers for prayer, comfort, and support. The body of Christ is the living expression of the Lord's love and compassion. Do not struggle by yourself—you are loved and not alone. Death will come, grief will grip your heart, but the God of all comfort will comfort you.

"All praise to God, the Father of our Lord Jesus Christ. God is our merciful Father and the source of all comfort."

2 CORINTHIANS 1:3, NLT

Heavenly Father, I lean into Your love and comfort in my inexpressible pain. Give me mercy and compassion to sit with those who are lingering with a terminal diagnosis. I'm grateful for the body of Christ as the living expression of Your love and compassion.

91

Trusting God on an Ordinary Day

Whoever dwells in the shelter of the Most High will rest in the shadow of the Almighty. I will say of the Lord, "He is my refuge and my fortress, my God, in whom I trust." Surely he will save you from the fowler's snare and from the deadly pestilence. He will cover you with his feathers, and under his wings will you find refuge; his faithfulness will be your shield and rampart.

PSALM 91:1-4

Often loss comes when we least expect it. We can wake up going about our business like it's just another ordinary day—until it isn't. On those days, our faith can be shaken. Yet it's especially during that time when we must trust God with everything we face. I'm reminded of when Lazarus became ill. His sisters sent word to Jesus, "Lord, the one you love is sick" (John 11:3). They expected Jesus to return to Bethany immediately, but Jesus stayed where He was for two more days. I can only imagine how Mary and Martha must have felt. There were probably moments when their faith and trust in Him wavered, and they wondered why Jesus didn't come immediately. But nothing comes as a surprise to God.

He always has a plan for us, and it's one we often know little about. If we trust in Him, eventually we will see Him turn our hardship and pain into something for our ultimate good. It's hard to see this through the eyes of loss and sadness. Our perspective is different from the Lord's. While we may never fully understand why things happen as they do, if we place our hope and trust in God, no matter what, He will make a way where there doesn't seem to be one.

"It is better to take refuge in the Lord than to trust in humans."

PSALM 118:8

Heavenly Father, help me to keep my eyes focused on You, especially on the days when I don't understand where You're leading me. I commit in my heart to trust You on the ordinary days, even when it appears differently than I had hoped.

92

Great Love, Deep Sorrow

They told him, "Lord, come and see." Then Jesus wept.

JOHN 11:34-35, NLT

Lazarus, a friend of Jesus and the brother of Mary and Martha, was deeply loved. The siblings grew up together playing, fighting, and having fun, but eventually they pursued more meaning in life by placing their faith in Jesus. These friends and family had grown especially close, and now they experienced the intense grief and sorrow of seeing one of them succumb to sickness unto death. Emotional and even angry, they wept together. Everyone who knew Jesus knew He could have healed His friend, but He didn't. First, He cried. After extending comfort, Christ brought Lazarus back to life, promising eternal life to all who believed.

Jesus is very clear that those who believe in Him, though they die, will live and never die. The Lord provides hope and healing for the heart now and for eternity. Trust in Him. Life is a pass-through that we get through—by prayer and God's people. Everyone's journey has joy and sorrow along the way. But peace is the outcome of receiving the Father's love, the Son's forgiveness, and the Spirit's comfort. Abide deeply in God's love to comfort your hurting heart. Weeping in the night is replaced by joy in the morning. A tearful heart looks to heaven's love.

"Weeping may last through the night, but joy comes with the morning."

PSALM 30:5, NLT

Lover of my soul, keep me close to Your heart and comfort my achy heart. When I lose someone, help me to remember that the greater my love for my lost loved one, the deeper my sorrow. But I praise You, the Man of Sorrows who is acquainted with my grief. Soothe my soul with Your love.

93

The Middle Miles

May the God of hope fill you with all joy and peace as you trust in him, so that you may overflow with hope by the power of the Holy Spirit.

ROMANS 15:13

Recently I was talking with a friend who is training for an Ironman. Although this isn't her first one, it will be her last. As we talked about the grueling training schedule and the commitment it takes to accomplish her goals, she told me about the middle miles. Apparently, those are the miles that are the most exhausting. The hardest part is not at the beginning of the race when you're fresh and feeling gung ho. Nor is it at the end when you can see the finish line in sight and know you will make it. The most difficult miles come mid-race, when your body is being tested to its limits, you're exhausted, and the excitement of the race is beginning to wane.

The grief journey is similar to this. Initially, many people gather around, bring food, check in daily, and help us through those difficult days. Then, after that, the calls become less frequent and everyone gets back to their own life. During these *middle miles*, we may feel alone and wonder how we got there. Yet, just like my friend, we must continue pushing forward, knowing we won't be in the middle forever. There will be a moment when we look up and see the sun again and can actually look back and see how far we have come.

"The Lord is my strength and my shield;
my heart trusts in him, and he helps me.
My heart leaps for joy, and with
my song I praise him."

PSALM 28:7

Jesus, how comforting it is to know You are with me across the middle miles of life. Even on those days when I question everything and everyone around me, I know I can always come back to You—my constant companion, my strength and support through every step along this journey.

94

Tears of Comfort

Jesus wept. Then the Jews said, "See how he loved him!"

JOHN 11:35-36

There is a non-verbal language of love that is communicated through compassionate tears. Empathy engages the heart at levels that verbal exchanges may not be able to penetrate. It is when someone responds to their emotions that a grieving soul senses they are cared for and understood. Tears quietly convey the aura of *I feel your pain—I hurt because you hurt.*

Comfort is the first step in seeking to serve someone in pain. Refrain from truth-telling until their heart receives proper care. Fear and anger have to be flushed from a hurting heart before facts can be appropriately applied and comprehended. It's from a context of love and acceptance that people trust and receive. Tears become a conduit for Christ's care.

We mourn with those who mourn so they know they are not alone. Desperation feeds at the table of aloneness, but security and peace preoccupy the person who is comforted by a community. It starts with a patient spouse or friend and spills over to sincere souls who trust in Jesus to bring wholeness and healing. Tears shed in love terminate isolation and invite intimacy. Replace shame with security in your Savior and trusting transparency with a caring community. Your tears open your heart to emotional and spiritual healing. Free your soul to speak with moist eyes to your master, Jesus, as He lovingly weeps with you.

"This is what the Lord, the God of your father David, says: I have heard your prayer and seen your tears; I will heal you."

2 KINGS 20:5

Precious Jesus, thank You for weeping with me and comforting me. Take my heart and hold it close to Your heart of peace. I trust Your love to wipe away my tears and fill me with the joy of my salvation. Fill my emptiness with the fullness of your grace, mercy, and love.

95

Tears: A Pathway to Healing Our Heart

Peace I leave with you; my peace I give you. I do not give to you as the world gives. Do not let your hearts be troubled and do not be afraid.

JOHN 14:27

Amid sorrow and mourning, perhaps you've wondered if the crying will ever cease. How many times did you think your tears were all dried up, yet out of nowhere, they began rolling down your cheeks for no apparent reason? In case no one has told you, this is perfectly normal in grief, and it's OK. Tears become our words when our heart is too shattered to express itself. If you're trying to keep a stiff upper lip and appear stronger on the outside than you actually feel on the inside, give yourself permission to be your beautiful, authentic self. This permission allows you to fully grieve without considering what others may think of you.

Letting go is like removing the chains you've wrapped yourself in. As Washington Irving said, "There is a sacredness in tears. They are not the mark of weakness but of power. They speak more eloquently than ten thousand tongues. They are messengers of overwhelming grief … and unspeakable love." Releasing your tears is healthy, as crying releases oxytocin and endorphins. These feel-good chemicals can help ease physical and emotional pain, giving you a sense of calm. Instead of looking at your tears as a sign of weakness, let's look at them as the love you have in your heart for the one your soul loves and longs for. Our tears truly are a pathway to the healing of our hearts.

"'But I will restore you to health and heal your wounds,' declares the Lord."

JEREMIAH 30:17

Heavenly Father, I place my broken heart within Your loving hands and know that You are the most gentle, loving, caring God. I know You see every tear and count each one. Thank You for saving them all and continuing to heal my brokenness.

96

A God Hug

Shout for joy, you heavens; rejoice, you earth; burst into song, you mountains! For the Lord comforts his people and will have compassion on his afflicted ones.

ISAIAH 49:13

A God hug is a timely gift. His hugs soothe, comfort, and calm. He is never late in offering His affection or too busy to stand still and embrace His human creation. The Spirit gently caresses burdened shoulders and rubs away our pain. His compassion has never failed. His mercy is fresh every day. Like a cool cream alleviates an itchy rash, so His balm of grace relieves a rash of worries. A God hug holds on until healing occurs. He holds on tight.

A God hug does not happen when we are on the run, but while we stand still. "Slow down, my child," He says. "Hush, I have this. Be still; let Me hold you. Rest in My arms." So we learn to stay stationary by faith and trust that the right activities will get done at the right time. When we schedule appointments to be loved by the Lord, we receive strength for the journey. Otherwise, we exhaust our ability to encourage without the infusion of Christ's courage. His hugs hearten.

Like the father of the Prodigal Son who came home, your Father in heaven can't wait to embrace you in your shame, stress, or success. He runs to greet you with warm acceptance, so throw yourself into His arms. Cast your cares on Christ and abandon your life to the Lord. Yes, enjoy His sweet embrace!

"I will turn their mourning into gladness; I will give them comfort and joy instead of sorrow."

JEREMIAH 31:13

Heavenly Father, I receive Your love and affection. Thanks for Your comforting hugs. Slow me down so I can be found by Your love and affection. By faith, I set my affections above with Christ, seated at Your right hand, praying on my behalf. Embrace me with Your hugs from above.

97

A Change in Perspective

So we fix our eyes not on what is seen, but on what is unseen, since what is seen is temporary, but what is unseen is eternal.

2 CORINTHIANS 4:18

Have you found that with significant loss comes a major change of perspective? Since losing your loved one, the things that were once so important are no longer. Death and grief bring about a major shift in our priorities. When death knocks on your door, your life changes in ways you never imagined. The things you once saw as being mountains have become molehills. There may have been a time when you were concerned with what others thought of you. Were you good enough? Smart enough? Thin enough? Pretty enough? Every day you wore a mask to hide your imperfections and cover up all the things you didn't want others to see. Now, those things are simply nonexistent.

We can't stay the people we once were, before our loved one died. This change in our perspective on life is like looking through the lens of a different pair of glasses. They are no longer cloudy or rose-colored. We realize how short life can be and how it can change in the blink of an eye. Our perspective is different; we can see more clearly now. As we view life through this new lens, we can become comfortable within ourselves, accepting that we are no longer the same people we once were. We will begin to learn how to live with who we are now.

"See, I am doing a new thing! Now it springs up; do you not perceive it? I am making a way in the wilderness and streams in the wasteland."

ISAIAH 43:19

Lord Jesus, help me to see my life through Your eyes and not through my eyes of sadness and sorrow. Looking at life through Your eyes will provide light where there is darkness, joy where there is sorrow. I know there is no way around it but through it, and I can only make it with You by my side.

98

The Fruit of Pain

Someone may be chastened on a bed of pain with constant distress in their bones, so that their body finds food repulsive, and their soul loathes the choicest meal … Let their flesh be renewed like a child's.

JOB 33:19-20, 25

A variety of spiritual fruit can be produced out of pain. We may gain a clear understanding of what breaks the heart of God. Sin may surface through the sieve of suffering that invites genuine contrition, confession, and repentance. Pain can be a symptom of a wound, self-inflicted or inflicted from an unfair situation or an insensitive person. Whether sin has entered the heart from the inside or from without, we must give it attention or it will erode the soul. Distress that draws us to God purifies our hearts.

Another fruit of pain is instruction from the Lord. It is an opportunity for God to instruct His children in a better way. A human being on his back is much more teachable than an individual running to and fro in frantic activity. We look up to heaven when we lie down face up, leveled by the forces of physical or emotional upheaval. Yes, our loving heavenly Father whispers intimate instructions to His loved ones who listen to His voice. Pain gives insight into God.

Allow your challenges to become a conduit to care for other hurting hearts. Channel your energy so you are not consumed by your cares alone, so that out of the depths of personal hurt you are able to bring the spirit of your sympathizing Savior Jesus to others. Consume the fruit of pain with your hungry heart, and your fruitful spirit can feed others who feel out of favor with God. Enjoy Christ's sweet comfort so you can comfort other hurting hearts.

"He will comfort us in the labor and painful toil of our hands caused by the ground the Lord has cursed."

GENESIS 5:29

Thank You, Lord, for Your pruning, instruction, and comfort. Give me the courage and strength to persevere through painful purging, so Your most luscious fruit can grow in my life. Use me to comfort the hurting, give hope to those who despair, and point people to Your love.

99

The Assumptions of Grief

"Peace I leave with you; my peace I give you. I do not give to you as the world gives. Do not let your hearts be troubled and do not be afraid."

JOHN 14:27

In the early days when we have lost someone we love, we feel as if our grief will last forever. Recovery seems hopeless, and we wonder what kind of God would allow us to remain in a perpetual state of sorrow. There are certain assumptions about grief that we have all heard, such as that there is a time limit for grieving, and after a certain number of months or certainly after one year, your grief should be gone. Another is that you should be the person you were before your loved one ran ahead to heaven. Or, how about this one: time heals all wounds. You'll get over it.

All of these assumptions are just that—assumptions. Although the essence of grief may last forever, there is a caveat that is important to know: Grief may last forever, but it does change over time. It evolves. The soul-crushing, heart-palpitating moments of grief lessen and eventually don't come as often. God is a God of love, and He longs to heal our broken hearts. We will one day make it through the valley of the shadow of death. We will carry our grief in our hearts forever, but know that it does change. You will push through the dark days—they will look different.

"May the God of hope fill you with all joy and peace as you trust in him, so that you may overflow with hope by the power of the Holy Spirit."

ROMANS 15:13

You, Lord, are the One who calms my fears and stills my heart when I begin to despair. You know that grief is as individual as our fingerprints, and You are patient and loving. Thank You for never leaving me to figure things out on my own.

100

Obey When Afraid

"Come," he [Jesus] said. Then Peter got down out of the boat, walked on the water and came toward Jesus.

MATTHEW 14:29

Sometimes Jesus sends us ahead in our boat of faith while He prays for us from a distance. We feel alone at times because He is not physically beside us to provide reassurance that we are on the right course. When global uncertainty or storms of sickness strike our core belief, we become fearful. In our crisis of faith, we can get out of our boat of fear and walk on the water toward Jesus or sink in unbelief.

Are you waiting to launch out in faith? Are you in the middle of a storm, anticipating His reassurance any minute? Or has He asked you to get out of the boat for a major faith-stretching goal? Wherever you are in your continuum of faith in Christ, trust Him in the transition. If you are on the shore, get in the boat of belief. If you are in the middle of one of life's fearful storms, look for Christ coming toward you. If He is asking you to get out of the boat and walk on water, trust Him. What seems unnatural or impossible to you may be reasonable to Him. It is not a blind leap of faith, for you are fixing your eyes on Jesus. Keep your eyes on Jesus. Do not look to the left at the storm, to the right at the still shore, or down at the swirling water. Look straight ahead into the confident eyes of Christ. Watch Him as you walk on water in faith.

"[Let us fix] our eyes on Jesus,
the pioneer and perfecter of faith."

HEBREWS 12:2

Dear Lord, how are You asking me to get out of my comfort zone and go with You? Give me the courage to obey instantly, even though I am not sure of the way. Replace my fears with Your tender touch. By faith, I clasp Your hand and hold on tight as we walk through rough waters.